Winning the Day Trading Game

John Wiley & Sons

Founded in 1807, John Wiley & Sons is the oldest independent publishing company in the United States. With offices in North America, Europe, Australia, and Asia, Wiley is globally committed to developing and marketing print and electronic products and services for our customers' professional and personal knowledge and understanding.

The Wiley Trading series features books by traders who have survived the market's ever-changing temperament and have prospered—some by reinventing systems, others by getting back to basics. Whether a novice trader, professional, or somewhere in-between, these books will provide the advice and strategies needed to prosper today and well into the future.

For a list of available titles, please visit our Web site at www.WileyFinance.com.

Winning the Day Trading Game

Lessons and Techniques from
a Lifetime of Trading

THOMAS L. BUSBY

WILEY

John Wiley & Sons, Inc.

Published by John Wiley & Sons, Inc., Hoboken, New Jersey.
Published simultaneously in Canada.

For general information on our other products and services or for technical support, please contact our Customer Care Department within the United States at (800) 762-2974, outside the United States at (317) 572-3993 or fax (317) 572-4002.

Wiley also publishes its books in a variety of electronic formats. Some content that appears in print may not be available in electronic books. For more information about Wiley products, visit our web site at www.wiley.com.

Library of Congress Cataloging-in-Publication Data

Busby, Thomas L., 1951–
 Winning the day trading game : lessons and techniques from a lifetime of trading / Thomas L. Busby.
  p. cm. — (Wiley trading series)
  ISBN-13: 978-0-471-73823-7 (cloth)
  ISBN-10: 0-471-73823-9 (cloth)
 1. Day trading (Securities) 2. Electronic trading of securities. I. Title. II. Series.
  HG4515.95.B87 2005
  332.63′228—dc22

                                                                    2005016420

ISBN-13 978-0-471-73823-7
ISBN-10 0-471-73823-9

Printed in the United States of America

Contents

Acknowledgments   vii

Introduction   ix

CHAPTER 1 The Crucible: Black Monday   1

CHAPTER 2 Time Is Central   15

CHAPTER 3 Trading Is a Numbers Game   31

CHAPTER 4 Read the Tape   45

CHAPTER 5 There's No Crying in Trading   61

CHAPTER 6 Riding the Rail   73

CHAPTER 7 Worry about Risk, the Rewards Will Come   85

CHAPTER 8 Respect the News   99

CHAPTER 9 Getting Down to Brass Tacks   113

CHAPTER 10 Preparation Pays   133

CHAPTER 11 A Study in Contrast   145

CHAPTER 12 Recap the Essentials   155

CHAPTER 13 An Afterthought for Consideration:
            The Doctrine of Genius   169

Appendix A Glossary   173

Appendix B Getting Started   179

Appendix C Order Types   185

Appendix D Suggested Reading   189

Appendix E Helpful Websites   191

Index   193

Acknowledgments

I would be remiss if I did not thank and acknowledge the people who helped me to write this book. First, I want to thank Paula, my wife of more than 20 years and my two sons, Winston and Morgan. I thank them not because they wrote the book but because they lived it. They know first hand what the life of a trader is like—they have ridden the rocky road with me and experienced the ups and the downs. I thank them for the chance to do the job I love. Their patience and understanding cannot be measured.

I also thank my Dad, Melvin. His guidance and instruction taught me the lessons that have been my guiding light throughout the years. They illuminated my path. Dad, I thank you.

Also, I want to thank Patsy Dow, my cousin, one of my students, and the wordsmith of this book. Patsy took my trading method and techniques and mixed them with my personal stories and experiences. She accurately transported them from my mind onto these pages. I appreciate her hard work and dedication to the task.

Thanks also to Jeanette Sims, the COO of DTI and my right hand. Jeanette spent many long hours proofing and editing these pages and adding her ideas to the mix. Geof Smith, our Chief Instructor at DTI created all of the artwork and graphics that enhance and explain the information presented. Thanks to a long-time friend and student, Christopher Castroviejo, who was instrumental in helping me with my facts, dates, and the overall structure of the content. Thank you to all of the DTI Students who have enchanced my education in the markets over the years. Thanks to all of you.

There is one other person who had a tremendous impact on my trading and that is Dr. Bobby Gene Smith. Over the years, he had such great faith in me and he was infinitely patient. He died a few years ago, but his influence in my life and the lives he touched was great.

Finally, a special thanks to Kevin Commins and all of the folks at John Wiley & Sons for allowing me the opportunity to publish this book.

Introduction

T rading is risky business that involves a great deal of discretion and skill. Accurate market analysis, correct execution, emotional control, discipline, consistency, and good money management are some of the skills that are required to trade successfully. In addition, there are times when any method, even when executed correctly, will result in a loss.

A great deal of effort has been made to insure that the information presented in this book is correct and accurate. However, we are all human and mistakes can always be made. The information and techniques presented have been helpful to me. However, I cannot and do not guarantee or assure you that they will work for you. I hope that you will find some of the ideas useful. In fact, I hope that your trading will be both more enjoyable and more profitable as a result of the information and ideas presented.

Before you trade, be sure that you can afford to lose the money that you are risking. Always limit your risk first and worry about taking profits second. I make money with this method, but past results are never a guarantee of future results.

Enjoy the book and trade with care.

CHAPTER 1

The Crucible

Black Monday

October 19, 1987. When the sun rose on that Monday morning, I felt financially secure. I had a great job, a beautiful house, nice cars, money in the bank, and a belief that the future would bring me greater and greater riches. By the time the sun set that evening, I was broke!

During the course of the day, the Dow Jones Industrial Average dropped more than 500 points. The Dow lost approximately 22 percent of its total value in a single day. One trillion dollars of financial assets vanished as quickly as a tiny puff of smoke in a strong wind. And, of course, the Dow was not alone. The Nasdaq also fell, losing more than ten percent of its value.

The United States financial markets underwent a free fall and there seemed to be no stopping, or even bracing, the fall. Furthermore, the decline was not limited to the United States. Major markets around the globe took a nosedive. It was as though a flame on Wall Street quickly got out of control and spread around the world faster than a fire in a parched, dense thicket. Close to home, the Canadian market reeled from historical losses and dropped over 20 percent before the disaster ended. The international scene was not any better: by the week's end, the average stock value on the London Financial Times Stock Exchange had declined by over 20 percent; Asian markets also tumbled. On October 20, the Nikkei experienced the biggest loss in its history. The market in Singapore was down significantly for the week. After experiencing a huge decline on October 20, the Hang Seng closed for days. In the wake of the crash, the Australian market suffered a record double-digit loss. Some exchanges and indices closed for a few days in the hope that the break or timeout would serve to calm jittery nerves. The reality of a global economy became all too real.

What caused the crash? Theories were cheap. Everybody had one. Program traders, soaring federal debt, high bond yields, market overvaluation—these were only a few of the speculated causes. In reality, all of these factors probably played a role. I didn't know the cause, and I really didn't care.

To me, the debate was strictly academic. What was real was that I, and some of my clients and dearest friends, had lost a lot of money. I had lost not only my wealth, but my self-confidence as well. I was broke and my faith in my trading ability was undermined. I grieved for my clients and for myself.

Even in the depths of my despair, there was no time for pity or resignation. I had a wife and two small children depending on me. It was time to be tested. Failure was not an option.

FROM PORK BELLIES TO PAN AM

At the time of the crash, I had been a trader for almost a decade. My experiences with the stock market began in 1978 when I was stationed in Spain with the U.S. Air Force. One of my fellow officers was trading pork bellies. He often talked to me about his experiences and the money he was making. He made it all sound very exciting and easy. I knew absolutely nothing about trading pork bellies or anything else, but I wanted a piece of the action. I did not have a clue as to how to begin, and the only brokerage firm I had ever heard of was Merrill Lynch. (This was back in the days when their major television advertisement was the bull in the china shop.) I truly thought that Merrill Lynch was the only brokerage firm in existence.

I was stationed at Torrejon Air Force Base in Madrid and the brokerage house was in the city's central business district. I had to use the subway, which I usually avoided because I found it so difficult. My Spanish was poor and my southern accent added a slow twang to the few Spanish words that I knew. Then, as now, I couldn't roll my tongue. In an effort to communicate, I gestured profusely. This small-town boy found downtown Madrid daunting. As I searched for the brokerage office, I just kept asking directions and gesturing. It was southern Spanish spoken with hand signals.

When I finally arrived at the office, I opened an equities account with the intention of trading pork bellies. I was so ignorant and naive that I didn't understand that pork bellies were a commodity and, therefore, couldn't be traded via a stock account. If you want to know the truth, I am not sure I even knew that pork bellies were commodities and equities were stocks. At any rate, I am sure that I did not have a clear view of the significant distinctions between the two.

Nevertheless, I opened an account. The military published *The Stars and Stripes*, a paper to boost the spirits of service people abroad and to help them stay in touch with events at home. I began following the financial information and paid close attention to the stock quotes, even though the quotes were about three days old. That was the extent of my market research. After reading *The Stars and Stripes* for a number of days, and considering the information presented, I decided to purchase my first stock. I bought 100 shares of Pan Am and another 100 shares of Eastern Airlines. I eagerly awaited every issue of *The Stars and Stripes* so that I could follow the fluctuating price of my holdings. It was exciting to be a stockholder and I enjoyed talking about my new portfolio.

Unfortunately, in the long run, my investments did not work out and both companies filed for bankruptcy. I had no stops; it was an all or nothing mentality. When both of my stock picks eventually went belly up, I lost everything from my first venture. However, I was not easily dissuaded. One loss did not make me a quitter. I enjoyed investing and I continued to study the markets looking for other stocks to purchase and other investment opportunities. Trading was the closest profession to sports that I had ever tried and I quickly gravitated to it. I had no idea that I would eventually become a professional trader. I just enjoyed the markets.

My Avocation Becomes My Vocation

After getting out of the military and returning to the United States, I settled in Oklahoma City and started attending law school. Trading for a living was not part of my life plan; in fact, I never even considered it. I intended to be a lawyer. I enrolled in law school while also continuing to invest in a small trading account. My trading was a hobby from which I hoped to eventually make a few bucks. My broker, Henry, and I soon developed a friendship and he introduced me to stock options in oil companies. At that time, oil was king in Oklahoma City. Henry taught me his trading strategy for options. It was a very easy three-step plan that he called the Bigger Fool Theory. The essence of the theory was simple: Buy a stock at a high price and there is always someone (a bigger fool) who will buy it from you at an even higher price.

Here is how the system worked. A stock price would rise one day, we bought it on the second day, and we sold it on the following day. I began regularly watching the market. Just as the strategy dictated, if an oil stock went up one day, I bought it on the second day, and then I sold it on the third day. Believe it or not, I successfully executed this strategy over and over again. Oklahoma City was booming and oil prices seemed to go up every day. The Bigger Fool Theory was working like a charm for me and my account was growing. I seemed to have a knack with options as evidenced by my profits. I didn't know that the odds of trading options to the long side were like playing the lottery.

One day I was surprised to receive an invitation to come to the local brokerage house and meet the boss. From the time I entered the door until the time I left the office, I was treated like royalty. I soon learned that the office manager was aware of my successful options trading. Everyone seemed to be impressed and they offered me a position. I was still attending law school and planned to finish my studies. I was not sure I wanted to be a broker or work in the financial field. I intended to be a lawyer. I communicated my feelings to them. However, the firm offered me a chance to achieve both objectives: accept the position with them and attend law school at night. I could be a broker in the Oklahoma City office and my studies would not be interrupted. It was an offer I could not refuse. I took the deal. From that day forward, my life would never be the same. I began the journey to becoming a trader. I started to educate myself about the stock market. I wanted to learn all of Wall Street's secrets.

Soon I received training in New York; not long thereafter I obtained my brokerage license and I returned to Oklahoma City where I honed my skills. I did well and gained the confidence of my clients and the management team at Merrill. I was dedicated to profitably managing my clients' portfolios and assisting them with their financial wealth management. I liked the industry and saw the potential to succeed and achieve my personal goals. Trading was both a passion and a profession for me. I loved it.

In 1982, the S&P Futures opened for trading. It was a watershed day for me. On that first day, I made the best and the worst single trade of my career. I bought the S&P at the open for a price of approximately 118.70. With the S&P currently trading at 1220.00, the trade would be worth $275,000.00 today! And that is just for one contract! That was my best trade ever because I have been buying it and selling it ever since. However, I also sold the S&P; that was my worst trade because if I had kept it, my investment would have yielded me incredible profits.

So, from the very beginning, I traded the futures indices. After studying futures, I added to my credentials by receiving a license to trade them. I quickly fell in love with this new market. As a beginning broker, I became concerned about the limitations of a one-way trading strategy. That is, if you buy stocks, you can only make a profit if the stock prices rise. But stocks move both ways. They go up and they go down. Therefore, the strategy that I had been taught was flawed. I knew I needed a strategy that worked in both bull and bear markets. Futures offered me the flexibility and the versatility that I needed. A stock trader with the best bull strategy in the world cannot profit from a bear market. Futures are not so restrictive. A good futures trader can make just as much money in a bearish market (maybe even more) than in a bull market. Trading opportunities are doubled. The trick is, of course, to correctly read the market and trade on the right side of it. That is where experience and education pay off.

I worked long hours and after four hard years, I was reaping the benefits. Within a short time I moved on and accepted a position with another established firm where I became a vice-president. I was one of the biggest producers in the office and, in fact, in the region.

Options became my obsession. You might say that I never met an option that I wouldn't sell. Just before the crash in 1987, I had assisted one of my largest clients in making over a million dollars in the options market. That is a million dollars of profit in one month! I was one of the biggest retail options traders in the United States. I thought I was one of the chosen. Walking on water didn't seem like that hard of a task. Then, came October 19, 1987, the day the floor evaporated beneath my feet.

My Mistake

I lost a lot of money on Black Monday. Let me tell you what happened. On Thursday, October 15, I was holding two contrary market positions. I was long 1000 S&P 100 puts and I was also short 1000 S&P 100 puts. My short position was offset by my long position and vise versa. There was no problem because the offsetting positions were my insurance against calamity. I was protected regardless of where the market traveled.

My problem surfaced on Friday the 16, just before the crash; my long positions expired but my short positions did not. They did not expire for another month; I was holding naked options. In other words, I had sold 1000 options that I did not own; I had guaranteed a buyer that I would deliver the options if the strike price was hit. On Black Monday the strike price was hit and I had to produce. Because I did not own the options, I was forced to buy them at a preset, high market price, even though the market was dropping like a ton of bricks.

If I had been able to hold onto my long puts for one more week, I would have made millions of dollars. But, the market did not wait for me. I was a day late and a thousand puts short. On Black Monday, with the market falling out of bed, all I could do was wring my hands and suffer. As the day progressed, I was literally throwing up in the trash can. That day, I experienced anguish that I never want to feel again.

THE AFTERMATH

I wish that I could say that on Tuesday, October 20, all was well for me, but that was not the case. I went to the office as usual, but the atmosphere in the office was far from usual. Our office was in turmoil. Throughout the financial industry there was total panic. Clients wanted to be assured that things were not so bad, but we could not offer that assurance. No one knew what that day or even the next day or week would bring. Everyone was asking questions. How much had been lost? Were we solvent? Were the markets going to continue to fall? Was the nation going to experience another depression like the one suffered in 1929?

Some analysts compared Black Monday of 1987 with Black Monday of 1929. Did the crash of 1929 cause the Great Depression? Was the world going to experience years of financial suffering? It depended on whom you read. Some writers predicted the worst while others framed the crash as nothing more than a correction. At any rate, a heavy sense of apprehension hovered over the financial industry. For a time, a sense of doom and dread engulfed the nation and the world.

Computer systems lacked the sophistication of the systems of today. So much information had been thrown at them so quickly that these titans of technology were not able to keep up and process the data. Over 600 million shares had traded hands on Black Monday alone. How bad was it? No one seemed to know. Wall Street firms feared the extent of their exposure. We were in quicksand and did not know what to do or where to begin to make sense of it. I remember selling some IBM shares and not knowing for days what my price was. It was clearly not the 2-second fill that we are accustomed to today.

The markets closed for a couple of days to evaluate the situation and to try to settle accounts. When the actual losses were calculated, it was an ugly sight. Those who refer to 1987 as a market correction always amuse me. Instantly, I know that they lack credibility. Black Monday was not a correction; it was a crash. On Monday, October 19, 1987, Wall Street experienced its greatest single-day loss to date. The loss dwarfed that of Black Monday in 1929. In 1929, the loss was only a little over 12 percent, but in 1987, the loss was over 22 percent. It was almost double. A correction? I don't think so. I, like many, many others, lost everything. I had to start over.

The financial loss that I suffered was catastrophic. However, believe it or not, that was not my biggest problem. My biggest problem was my loss of self confidence. I questioned my experience and my ability to trade. How could I not have seen what was coming? How did I let this happen to me? Was I to blame for the suffering of my family, my clients, and me? Should I have done things differently? What should and could I do now?

Over the next few weeks and months, I had to undergo a lot of soul searching. I questioned the basis and the rationale of the financial institutions that had been my source of livelihood for years. And, I questioned whether or not I had foolishly selected a profession in which years of work and labor could vanish in a single day.

Survive and Persist

As I thought about my plight, I remembered the struggles I had when I tried out for my high school football team. My nemesis was a big brute named Danny. At every practice, I had to face Danny. When we collided, my bones rattled and my brains shook. He must have weighed well over 200 pounds and he was as solid as a slab of granite. I was a freshman in high school hoping to make the team, and Danny, a soon to be all-state lineman, had made it his goal in life to peal my face, one layer at a time. Day after day, Danny tackled me—violently exhibiting his superior gridiron skills. When I saw that mountain coming at me, I had one thought: survive the blow. I braced for the impact. After I survived, I had another thought: flee. Quit. Forget about playing football. It is just too hard, and I don't need the hassle. Danny was deadly.

I tried to convince my Dad to see it my way. I told him that I should quit. I explained to him how hard it was. I told him how big this other guy was and how humiliated I felt to be pulverized by him day after day. I promised to study more, work harder, be a better human being, but Dad would have none of it. "Don't start something that you're not going to finish. You wanted to join the football team. You went out for it and now you are going to finish it. You will not be a quitter." So day after day I faced the mountain.

When tryouts ended, no one was more surprised than I was that I had made the team. I was not an all-star and I took my turn warming the bench, but I was on the team. Persistence had paid off and I wore the team uniform with pride.

On October 20, 1987, and for many, many days thereafter, I felt like that young high school freshman who was being battered by that mountain of a lineman. The air had been knocked out of me. I had to fight to survive. I wanted to quit trading, but I needed the money. I was a victim of the crash of 1987. That is the way I viewed myself. The market had victimized me. It had behaved in an irrational and inexplicable manner and it did so intentionally to hurt me. It was personal. Rationally, I knew that was not true, but I wanted to blame someone or something. I felt sorry for myself. I was literally drowning in self-pity.

Additionally, I was also having a lot of conflicts with my employer. They approached my clients as numbers and I considered my clients as friends. The office environment had become very unpleasant and stressful. I had to make a change. I needed to move on. I decided that I should leave my position and find employment elsewhere, but where? I had to have a new position that gave me the ability to provide for my family. What type of position should I seek? Should I stay in the financial field or practice law, or business, or something else? One thing was sure, I had to make a living somehow. My life was flipping upside down and I seemed to have no center or direction. It is difficult to relate the depth of despair that I felt.

I had not been raised with money. My father was a civil servant who made a modest income and provided for me sufficiently, but there were few frills. Dad had a well-deserved reputation for being thrifty and he usually pinched a penny until it squeaked. Growing up, if you didn't need to turn on a light, you left it off. If you turned it on, you turned it off when you left the room. Wastefulness was a sin and you didn't waste food, clothes, utilities, gas, money, or anything else. Sears or J. C. Penney was a fine place to shop, and eating out or going on a vacation was an extravagance. Dad saved as much as he could; he saved a little from every paycheck. He managed his finances well and always prepared for that inevitable rainy day. Now it seemed that he had managed far better than I had. I was totally unprepared for the rain that pelted down on me. I was a Bozo and I felt it to my core. I asked myself over and over again: How could this be happening to me?

As an adult, I had become accustomed to living well. I bought what I wanted, at least most of the time. My family lived in a beautiful home. We drove new cars. My children attended private school. My wife had furs and jewelry and other trappings of the financially comfortable. Then, overnight, my family and I had to give up the luxuries we enjoyed and settle for far, far less. It was psychologically very difficult.

Once you have had money and lose it, it is painful. It is not just giving up the big house and other such stuff. I'm not so spoiled that I can't drive an older model car. But, it is the psychological effect of failure. I felt like the world's biggest fool. I had spent time and money educating myself. I had a law degree, a degree in business, training in the military, and a good upbringing that stressed good money management. Yet, here I was in the worst financial situation of my life. How did I let it happen? I just kept asking myself that question over and over again. My self-confidence was just south of zero!

Just like on that football field when I had come face-to-face with that big lineman, my first thought was for survival. I liquidated everything I could. The house, the cars, the investment portfolio—just about anything marketable was sold. Still, there was not nearly enough money. I started going into debt and relying heavily on credit cards. I worked hard to appear to be okay, and that just added to the pressure. It is exhausting to try to look like all is well when you know that your sky is falling. I was probably technically bankrupt, but I never declared bankruptcy. Declaring bankruptcy was simply not an option. I never really considered it. I continued to struggle and hoped to find a way out of the deep pit where I found myself. I was not a quitter.

I always was an optimist, happy with my life and my achievements. I had believed that good guys always win and that my future would just get better and better. Now, the man in the mirror was a confirmed pessimist. He expected the worst, and he was getting it.

Oklahoma City had weathered the Penn Square Banking Crisis and the oil crash. Yet, now there were few opportunities in the city for me. I decided to leave the west and head south. I returned to my hometown of Mobile, Alabama. I went to work for E. F. Hutton and received enough money to get on my feet. The bulk of that money was eventually lost by investing in a company recommended by an associate. Once again, my ignorance cost me. I did not do enough analysis and I put all of my eggs in one basket.

As luck would have it, during this period of time in the brokerage community, consolidation and mergers were very common. Unfortunately, E. F. Hutton was soon to be no more. That particular opportunity was gone and I basically started looking for any viable opportunity to earn a few bucks.

By day, I continued to trade the S&P Futures. I traded very small positions and lost money far more often than I made it. My outlook on life was so dark and dismal that I expected my trading to fail and it did. As I look back, I realize that my attitude was a tremendous detriment to my trading. I tried to improve. I studied technical analysis as well as various charting techniques, wave theories, and patterns. I read every trading book I could find. I desperately wanted to make money in the markets because I knew there were millions to be made, but nothing seemed to work for me. From 1987 until 1992, I worked incredibly hard but had nothing to show for it. Now, I realize that it is not about working hard; it is about working smart.

I looked for other financial opportunities and by night I worked with a group of men to manage some funds for a local tribe of Native Americans. We experienced some small success, but that was not the answer. We put together some capital and actually opened a casino in Biloxi, Mississippi, but that, too, was not the panacea. Every day of my life had become a fight for my survival. I call these years my dark years.

Trading is a very psychological game. If you are under too much stress or if you are too fearful and pessimistic, you cannot trade successfully. That point was driven home to me on a daily basis as I lost on trade after trade after trade. After every loss, I considered quitting, but every time I remembered my Dad admonishing me to stick it out. "If you can't finish it, don't start it."

Everyday I had to tell myself again that I was not a quitter. Things would get better. I just did not know how or when. Trading is a journey: You learn as you go and I was doing a lot of learning.

The Metamorphosis Begins

Sometimes you experience an event that has a profound effect on you. You can't explain why, but it just does. You may have had similar experiences that didn't even faze you, but for some reason, this time it's different. The experience speaks to you in a unique and dramatic way and it impacts your life.

If you have ever tried to quit smoking or lose weight you probably know what I mean. You were well aware that you were fat. You knew rationally that you needed to lose weight because those pounds were adversely affecting your health. You even knew how to get rid of those excess pounds. Proper nutrition was not foreign to you and you could recite dozens of diets by heart. But you just could not lose weight or stick to any diet. In fact, you probably got fatter every time you tried to reduce the number on the scale because you were not buying into the need or the way to change.

Then one day you heard or saw something that you had heard or seen dozens of times before. And for some unknown reason, you finally got it. You began eating a balanced diet, living a healthy lifestyle, and losing weight. On that particular day you were ready for the message you received and you took it seriously and changed.

In 1992, I had a far more significant life-altering experience. I didn't shed a few pounds; I shed five years of misery.

The Sermon

My wife Paula, our two sons, and I went to the Sunday service as usual. George Mathison may have been the minister of a small Methodist church, but his ministerial skills were far from small. He was well versed in the scriptures, extremely articulate, and very personable. When he spoke, you felt as though he was speaking to you individually. George could preach one heck of a good sermon.

On this particular day, I was anticipating going through the motions of worship; singing a few well-known hymns, listening to some good words of encouragement, and leaving for another tough week ahead. Things started off as planned. The music was good and George began the sermon. However, when I heard his voice, things changed quickly. This message was not just good, it was great, and it was tailor made for me. George was talking about forgiveness and allowing God to share life's burdens with you. He was talking about forgiving yourself and giving your burdens to someone far stronger than you will ever be. I was encouraged. Could I allow myself the freedom to give my load to God and let God help me gain a new freedom from the baggage I was carrying?

The weight had been so heavy for so long. Not one day had passed since 1987 that I had not revisited my mistakes. I had carried the guilt of that experience like a load of heavy metal welded to my being. I trudged through every day because my burden was so heavy. Could I put that burden down? Could I forgive myself and be free? I listened more intently.

George was urging me to forgive myself for my sins and my mistakes. "If God can forgive you, surely you can forgive yourself." I was so hungry for this message. I wanted to quit calling myself a Bozo and move on with my life. I had tried, but I had been unable to do it. Now, there was hope. I leaned forward in the pew, not wanting to miss a word.

I don't remember exactly what he said, but I remember the essence of it. Or, at least the kernels of wisdom that I took from it: Life is full of problems that are often so great that they overwhelm us. We want to solve them alone and we want to solve all of them instantly. But we can't. No one can deal with all of the problems of life without help. Sometimes our load is too heavy; but if we share our difficulties with God and allow him to help us, he will. We can give our burdens to God and free ourselves from the guilt and the pain that we are suffering.

I had not sinned in 1987, but I had made mistakes. I wanted to hear more. George continued: First, give the baggage of the past to God. Then, deal with life's problems from this day forward one at a time. All a human being can do is the best he or she can do. No one can climb a mountain with one step, or cross an ocean with one row of a paddle. No one can find a solution to every one of life's problems in one fell swoop —and neither can you. Let God forgive you for your shortcomings and forgive yourself. Then take life one day at a time and do the very best that you can do on that day. Some days you will do well and some days you won't do so well. Just focus on doing the very best that you can. Solve the problems you can solve and handle the situations that you can handle that day. That is all that you can do. No human being is expected to do more than that.

This advice may seem simplistic, but from my point of view, it was not. I knew that I needed to set myself free and then to take one problem at a time, one day at a time, and one trade at a time. I did it. I put that burden down. I gave it to God and I felt a sense of freedom that I had not felt in years.

Then George's message concluded with a suggestion. At the end of every day, after you have done the best that you can do, reset yourself. Think of your day as a message on a tape recorder. Visualize yourself as having a reset button in your head. At the end of the day, reset the button. The day is over. You cannot change it. Take everything positive from it that you can, and move on. Begin the next day with a clean slate and with a determination that in the course of the new day, you will again do your best.

I'm sure that the message was more eloquently presented. It must have been persuasive because that experience changed me. It altered the way I have conducted myself from that day until this one. I started doing things differently. According to Paula, I even walked differently. I carried myself more erectly and there was lightness in my step. I put the burden down. I no longer carried it alone. Believe it or not, when I left that sermon I had a new perspective. I stopped beating myself about my past mistakes. I started looking at the present and taking each day as a new chance to do my best.

When I walked outside, I suddenly noticed that it was a perfect spring day. The sky was brilliantly blue and the grass was a deep rich green. Spring was here and azaleas, daffodils, and tulips were blooming everywhere. The ride home was so beautiful. I heard the birds singing and I felt carefree.

I applied George's message to every aspect of my life. My approach to trading dramatically changed. I began looking at the market differently. The baggage from the past had been shed. I stopped imposing my old views on the market and started listening to what the market was telling me. I was no longer a pessimist. I was optimistic again.

At the end of each trading day, I started analyzing my trades and trying to learn from them. If some or all of them were losers, I studied them hard and questioned why I had entered those particular trades. I tried to determine what indicators might have tipped me off that I was on the wrong side of the market and I pondered why I had misread those indicators. I looked hard at the winners, too. How could I have made more money? How could I have done even better? Then I asked myself the big question. Regardless of whether I won or lost, did I do the best that I could do as a human being and as a trader? I tried hard to always be able to answer the question with a "yes." I never intended to make mistakes in my life or in my trading. I always did the best I could and I always used the best analysis that I could with my trading. If I had made mistakes, I put them down. I reset that button in my head and let that day go.

When I begin each trading day, I begin with a fresh start and with one goal in mind: to be the best trader and the best person that I can be during the course of the day. I will make mistakes. We all do, but I don't worry about yesterday. I learn from my mistakes. Yesterday is gone. Today is the challenge. My goal is to be the best trader that I can be today.

Focus on Managing Risk First and Taking Profits Second

Black Monday sucker punched me, but I got back up. The psychological pain was far worse than the pain inflicted by that all-state lineman in high school. But I did not quit. I stuck it out and my perseverance paid off. For many years, just thinking about October 19 made me ill. Little did I know that almost 20 years later, I would consider it the best thing that ever happened to me.

My focus turned to managing the risk and taking profits became secondary. As any trader or investor knows, where there is the possibility of great reward, there is also the reality of great risk. One of my favorite trading vehicles is futures and many analysts consider futures inherently risky.

To the uneducated trader, that is true. Futures are highly leveraged trading instruments that allow skillful traders to make a lot of money and unskillful traders to be fleeced. Therefore, I had to design a strategy for managing my risk while trading futures. Later chapters discuss the specifics of my method, which came straight from the school of hard knocks. The most significant thing is that after Black Monday, risk management became the single most important element of my trading.

Out of my darkest days, I developed a trading method that allows me to limit my risks and protect my capital while maximizing my profit-making potential. I am truly a day trader. I get into the market, get my money or suffer my loss, and get out. I rarely hold large positions long term, never hold futures contracts long term, and I never leave positions in the market when I am unable to monitor them.

There is no crying in trading. I take full responsibility for my actions in the marketplace. I never blame anyone else for my failures. I make my trading decisions and I accept the results. The majority of the time, I am happy with my bottom line.

Throughout the course of this book, I share some of my techniques. I explain to you the significance of using a global trading approach; I identify and explain the indicators I monitor. I explain how I control risk and how I maximize profits. I also detail the equipment needed to begin to trade electronically and the steps involved in getting started.

Trading can be a very risky business. Before you risk your first dollar, be sure that you educate yourself. Never risk money that you cannot afford to lose. There are many courses and programs that teach you how to trade. In 1996, with the encouragement of one of my longtime friends and clients, I began the Day Trading Institute (DTI), a trading school in Mobile, Alabama. I am dedicated to teaching the art of trading. If at the end of my work day I have helped one person escape the failures I endured and trade this market profitably, then I consider that day a success.

Realize that my method is not the only method that works. Other methods may work for you. The key is to learn a market-tested strategy and learn how to execute it. This book is not a substitute for proper education and training. It is merely an introduction to the methods that I use and teach. There is so much more to learn. Successful traders continuously learn and adapt to changing market conditions. If you are a systems trader, I have to tell you that there is no Santa Claus. The market changes; what doesn't change is the people and human nature.

If you are a beginner, take it slow. In fact, do not begin until you are certain that you know the risks involved and you have the financial resources to suffer the consequences of any actions you take. I hope that some of my techniques prove helpful to you. Trading is not easy but the educated trader can win. Be a winner!

LESSONS LEARNED

- Be persistent. Study the game.
- Don't worry about yesterday. Focus on today.
- Educate yourself. The uneducated lose.
- Risk management must be your first priority. Do not risk money you cannot afford to lose.
- Learn from every trade. Analyze and critique yourself continuously, but always trade in the present.

CHAPTER 2

Time Is Central

I 've never been much of a fisherman, but my grandmother loved to fish. I remember her sitting on the bank of a creek in rural Tuscaloosa, Alabama. She sat patiently with her checked dress draped across her knees and her old straw hat protecting her eyes from the intensity of the sun. She didn't always fit the part, but she was as dedicated to her task as any angler has ever been. She rested her long cane pole across her lap; stared intently at the water, and waited. Often, she sat almost motionless for hours anticipating a bobble from her cork that would signal her catch. When suppertime arrived, the rewards of waiting were clear. A big plate of fried brim, hot and tasty, sat in the center of the table with some good homemade cornbread and fresh vegetables.

Like fishing, trading is also a waiting game. Jesse Livermore, one of Wall Street's trading legends wrote, "It's not the thinkin' that makes the money—it's the sittin' and the waitin' that makes the money." According to Richard Smitten, Livermore's biographer, Livermore knew the significance of time. He studied the market intently to find the right moment to buy or sell. He did not jump on just any trade; he watched and he waited. He knew that his caution would cause him to miss some chances to make money, but he did not care because he also knew that the market offers many more occasions to play a winning hand. Livermore believed that timing is everything. If you enter the market too early or too late, you can lose money. There is an ideal opportunity for entry; you have to be patient until you see it. Livermore was extremely astute at picking the right time and his acumen earned him the title of the Greatest Bear on Wall Street. (*How to Trade In*

Stocks, Jesse Livermore. with adapted materials by Richard Smitten. See also *The Amazing Life of Jesse Livermore*, Richard Smitten.)

Trading is exhilarating and down-right fun. Sometimes we have to remind ourselves that we are not trading just for the pleasure of it. We are trading to make money. I do not trade for sport. I play golf for sport. I trade to make a living. Like my grandmother, I want the fish to be biting. If they are not, I sit, watch, and get ready. I know that the market will offer many opportunities to make money. I just have to correctly identify them.

IN THE MARKETS, JUST LIKE FISHING, PATIENCE PAYS

One of my dearest friends and clients, Dr. Bobby Gene Smith, taught me many useful lessons about life and about trading. In the early 1980s, Dr. Smith and I bought stock in a company called Pre-Paid Legal (PPD). We only paid one dollar a share for the stock. After our purchase, the stock price began to rise and it just kept going higher and higher. On a number of occasions, I met with Dr. Smith and during the course of the meeting we always talked about our Pre-Paid Legal stock and what we wanted to do with it. Consistently, I wanted to sell and he wanted to hold. When our profit margins doubled, I really wanted to sell and I encouraged him to do so, but he had other ideas. He was in no rush to take fast profits. "Just be patient, Tom. Be patient and wait a little longer." That was always his reply.

Eventually the stock price hit $20.00 per share. Then, and only then, did Dr. Smith agree to sell. His patience paid us both handsomely. Patience does pay. Dr. Smith correctly identified the ideal time to liquidate our holdings.

CAREFULLY SELECT TRADING OPPORTUNITIES

How do successful traders know when to trade? Of course there are many different answers based on various methods and strategies. As for me, I ask myself one central question. Should I be long, short, or out of the market? Experience taught me that if I consistently answer the big question right, I make money. If I consistently answer it wrong, I lose money. It is that simple and yet that complex. If I cannot answer the question with a high degree of certainty, or if I determine that I should be out of the market, I wait. I sit on the sidelines, observe, and gather data. I look for the right opportunity when the odds favor my success.

As seasoned traders know, answering the big question accurately is the tricky part. The financial markets are in a constant state of flux; they are up one minute and down the next. Some days are worse than others. Take June 17, 2005, for example, it was an options closeout day and the market was more unpredictable than usual. I made money in the early session, but I stayed out in the afternoon when the market stagnated. Had I traded all day long, I would very likely have lost money. Pick your trading battles carefully to avoid unnecessary losses.

Because the market continuously changes, every trader must have a proven strategy to win. If you do not have a proven method, you will jump in and out of the market with every dip and upswing. I know because I have done it.

Believe it or not, I remember one day when I traded from the time the market opened until the final bell rang. When I tallied up my trades, I had executed about 3000 transactions. At that time, placing so many trades in a single day was not easy to do because the industry wasn't as computerized as it is today. Orders had to be called into the desk. But, somehow, I managed to keep the lines hot. At the close of the session, I thought I had done well. I had been right more times than I had been wrong and I expected my account to show it. I anxiously awaited my profit totals. To my surprise, when I received my statement, my account showed a loss because I forgot to calculate the commissions and other costs associated with the huge volume of trades that I was making. In those days, you received a confirmation sheet for each trade. When the confirmation records from that day arrived, they stood almost a foot high. I worked hard all day to lose money. Never forget the reason that you are trading. You are trading to make money!

One of my friends and a professional trader once advised me that traders should limit their trades to prevent errors. As simple as it sounds, by limiting the number of trades, you immediately reduce the number of times that you must be right. My rule is to never execute more than six different trades during any 24-hour period. Over trading is typically not profitable trading. Just because you trade a lot doesn't mean that you will make a lot of money.

So how do you know whether to be long, short, or out of the market?

Over the years, I developed a strategy that keeps me from over trading and helps me to stay on the right side of the market most of the time. The foundation of my strategy consists of three basic elements: time, key numbers, and market indicators. I also use a multiple contract approach that lets me take some early profits while keeping a portion of my position to follow the daily trend. In this chapter, I explain how I use time and how my timing strategy helps me to make money. Later chapters concentrate on other aspects of my trading method, and I share some of the insights that I gained from a lifetime of trading.

CERTAIN MARKET MOVEMENTS CORRELATE TO THE TIME OF DAY

In 1992, when I looked at the markets with a new perspective, I saw things that I had not seen before. I had new faith and confidence in the rationality of both life in general and of Wall Street in particular. With my renewed faith came a new determination to study and better understand the financial world. I looked closer at the futures markets and tried to find something that was constant about them. I was like a scientist conducting an experiment. I wanted a control; a place where I could hang my hat and begin to study other factors and variables. Even more significantly, I truly believed that I could develop a trading strategy to make some real money; the world was no longer a hostile place.

I watched the markets day after day and hour after hour. At first glance, almost everything seemed to be continuously changing. I was looking for something that would be the same on Friday that it was on Monday, and that would be the same in December as it had been in January. Once I found that constant, I would begin to build a strategy around it. I found that constant to be time.

Simply stated, people are creatures of habit. People move the market. Every working day our lives follow the same basic time patterns. Most of us wake up and get to work around 8:00 A.M. or so. We work several hours and break for lunch. After eating, we again return to the office and finish the day. Traders follow the same pattern as everyone else. Around 8:00 A.M., they begin observing the markets. When the markets open, they dive into their day and there is a lot of buying and selling as they jockey for their daily positions. The volume in the markets reflects this peaked interest. For a couple of hours the markets tend to be very active translating into liquidity and volatility.

After working for a while, traders, just like most folks, get hungry; they want to take a break for lunch. Around 10:30 A.M. (Central Time), the volume drops as brokers and traders start preparing for lunch. Noon approaches and on Wall Street and across the U.S. traders sit down at a restaurant or a table in the office to enjoy lunch. They are not placing orders and consequently, volume drops; reflecting the lost interest.

After the lunch break, folks return to work and the activity begins again. Volume usually picks up and there is more action. In midafternoon, bonds close and there is a brief period when things get relatively quiet. Finally, just before trading ends for the day, there is another flurry of activity as many traders liquidate their positions. Perhaps they know they are on the wrong side of the market and have to get out of losing trades, or in some cases, they do not want to stay in the market overnight. At any rate, there is another intensified band of buying and selling near the close.

Correlate trading to the time patterns of the majority of traders and you have one of the most significant keys to trading. It may sound simplistic, but it is a really big thing. Select a market and observe it for a few days. Notice when and how it moves during the course of a day or an entire week. You will see, as I did, that there are certain market trends, both long term and short term, that are connected to time. This observation led me to the realization that time is one of the most important elements in trading.

I use the concept of time in a variety of ways and the following explains how and why I do it.

Active Times Are Best for my Trading

To make money when trading, it is essential to have liquidity and volatility. Liquidity is necessary because you need it to enter and exit the market. Without liquidity, you may be forced to hold a position far longer than you wish. When that happens, your assets are tied up and you can't take advantage of other, more profitable opportunities. Therefore, the liquidity of an asset is vital, especially to a day trader who needs to have the ability to get in and out of the market quickly.

Volatility is also very important. What good does it do to buy or sell a stock, futures contract, or any other asset if the asset does not move up or down? Once you get into a transaction, the market needs to move in your favor quickly so that you can take some profits. Never forget that making money is the name of the game.

I remember one painful night when I ignored the significance of liquidity and volatility. It was the Thanksgiving holiday and I was bored. You have to understand that I love to trade and I like playing the game. My boredom led me to get into the night market. It wasn't a smart thing to do, but I did it.

Some folks mistakenly think that the markets are closed on all holidays, nights, and weekends. That is not so. Technology offers the educated trader an opportunity to trade virtually 24-hours a day—even on many holidays.

So, while other people were eating turkey, I was trading. In fact, I put on a very large position. The market was extremely quiet; my boredom got me stuck in a stagnant market. As the evening hours passed, I tried to go to bed and rest. But, my position was so large that I could not go to sleep. I had to keep monitoring the market. I was forced to stay in the trade for 12 hours because I ignored my rules regarding timing.

You do not want to do as I did and get stuck in a market that is going nowhere. Active markets provide the money making opportunities that successful traders need. These are the times that are the most fertile for making money.

Morning Activity Can Create Ideal Trading Conditions

I do a lot of trading in the morning and I often trade the S&P 500 Futures Index. Therefore, I use that market to explain my most lucrative trading times. Trading in the open outcry pits of the S&P Futures opens each morning at 8:30 A.M., Central Time. (Please be aware that I live in Mobile, Alabama and the times I use in this book are all Central, unless specifically stated otherwise.) Initially, the market is highly volatile. Typically, it jumps around quite a bit for the first five to ten minutes. Watch and wait. Don't leap into the S&P or any other market at its open because you do not have a clear picture of where it is going. Be a spectator until it settles down and you are able to get a real sense of its intended direction. In some cases it is probably a good idea to give the futures markets a good 30 minutes or so to calm down. It is often said that amateurs open the market and the professionals close it. Don't be one of the amateurs who prematurely put their money at risk.

After the market has a chance to settle, it is generally a good time to trade. I like to trade between 9:00 A.M. and 10:15 A.M. During the first two hours of trading, I am often able to get into a trade, take some profits, and position myself to take advantage of the day's trading trend. I explain my multiples method and how I position myself for what I call a free ride later. For now, just picture the opportunity to control a huge amount of equity while positioning your risk to break even.

As the morning hours pass, volume falls off and trading becomes very slow. This is not always true, but it is most of the time. Around 10:15 A.M., I walk away from my computer and do other things. If you sit in front of your computer all day long, unless you have tremendous discipline, you will overtrade and your profitability will suffer. I do not generally place any new orders during this time. Due to the usually slower movement of the major exchanges, trading becomes riskier for my method. I know that there will be safer times and I wait for them.

If I am in a trade from earlier in the morning, I check to make sure that I have a protective stop in place and I leave it. If the market is signaling a reversal, I may exit my positions entirely and take my profits. But, I rarely place new orders between 10:15 A.M. and 12:30 P.M. The risks are stacked against me during this time because with reduced volume comes less predictability. There will be better opportunities. The market is full of opportunities and I wait for them.

Sometimes my caution causes me to miss out on good trades. But so what? I do not need to make every trade. If most of my trades are winners and I practice good money management, I will be okay.

Afternoon Trading Offers Additional Opportunities

After lunch, I look at the market again. Twelve-thirty P.M. is a very important trading time. It is a pivotal time because, after lunch, the market tends to reset and either reverse the morning move or accelerate it. The 12:30 P.M. number is so important that I record it and use it as a major pivot for the next 24 hours. If the market trades above the 12:30 P.M. number, it signals a bullish move. If it trades below the 12:30 P.M. number, it signals a bearish move. Of course, I consider the 12:30 P.M. pivot as only one factor among others, but it is an important number to watch.

One of my cardinal rules is that I never go short between 12:30 P.M. and 1:00 P.M. Too often, the market appears to be going down during this time, but the move is not long lasting. I was burned far too often by shorting the market during this time frame. Sometimes it is quite tempting, but I hold firm. If I want to short the market, I wait until after 1:00 P.M. If I am already short going into 12:30 P.M., I make sure that my stop is in a good place and see if the trade continues through to 1:00 P.M. But I will not initiate a new position on the short side between 12:30 P.M. and 1:00 P.M. The market taught me this lesson and forced me to listen.

If you trade in the afternoon, you need to be aware of a time that I consider to be very dangerous for most traders. Often between 1:30 P.M. and 2:00 P.M. there is a counter trend. Sometimes this trend can be rather dramatic and the market becomes extremely volatile and unpredictable. At DTI, we refer to this time segment as the Grim Reaper because traders caught in it may see the demise of their trade. Generally, I avoid trading during this time. It just is not worth the pain.

The End of the Session Creates a Final Flurry

The third and final time during the trading day that I frequently trade is near the daily close. The S&P Futures closes at 3:15 P.M. As the market nears the end of the session, the daily trend may reverse. If the market has been down for the bulk of the day, it may shift up. Or, if it has been an up day, the market may seek lower prices and squeeze out those traders who are long. This trading time can be very lucrative because many traders have to liquidate their positions before the close, and if you are educated, you can take advantage of that fact. It all boils down to key numbers, time, and the RoadMap indicators—long, short, or out?

Trade Zones

To simplify my trading, I identified certain periods throughout the trading day when I look for opportunities. I refer to these time frames as trade zones. Based on the trading patterns of most traders as explained previously, I generally place most of my trades during the following times:

Trade zone one   9:00 A.M.–10:15 A.M.
Trade zone two   12:30 P.M.–1:15 P.M.
Trade zone three   2:15 P.M.–2:45 P.M.

That is not to say that I never trade outside these zones. If the market direction is very clear, I may enter the market at 8:45 A.M., but I very rarely enter between 10:15 A.M. and 12:30 P.M. or between 1:15 and 2:15 P.M. The waters are just too treacherous and I do not like throwing my money away. Also, if I am in the market at the end of a trade zone, I may hold my position, but, I keep a protective stop in place to prevent me from taking a beating if there is a sudden market shift.

Again, let me stress that I designate these times as trade zones because my multiple contract trading method works best during times of greatest liquidity and volatility. When the market is not moving and when there is low volume, I generally do not want to be in the market. Why would I? There is no need to risk my money unless the chances are good that I will be able to make money.

USE A 24-HOUR TRADING CLOCK

Just because I limit the majority of my trading during the day to trade zones, does not mean that I do not monitor the market and even do some trading during other significant times. I developed a software program several years ago called The RoadMap. It allows me to track markets around the clock. There are, of course, other programs that you can use to accomplish this same objective, but without the detail. I always keep tabs on the German DAX and trade it often in the early morning hours before the U.S. day market opens. Not only do I trade the DAX, but I also use it and other foreign markets to help me with my night trading when I am trading the S&P and the Dow. The method I teach focuses on how to use a 24-hour trading clock.

There is no question that the United States is the world's financial leader. Living in the United States, it is all too easy to take a provincial view and focus all attention on exchanges and indices located in Chicago or New York City. However, the world is a big place and there are other extremely important geographical areas that we need to watch. Savvy traders keep an eye on markets in Europe and Asia. Foreign markets offer both trading opportunities and insight that can help us to trade more profitably.

Globally, trading follows the movement of the sun. The geographical part of the world where the sun is shining will be the part of the world where trading is most active. Until recently, that fact did not mean much to the United States, home-based trader. However, thanks to major strides in technology, traders now sit in their bedroom or in an office and follow the Nikkei, the Hang Seng, the DAX, and other foreign exchanges or indices. In fact, with the right platform and account, it is possible to trade some of these markets. I regularly trade the DAX.

Technological advances opened a big, new world of electronic trading opportunities. A few years ago, the average trader could not trade the night markets electronically without a very expensive Globex terminal, or otherwise he had to place all orders through the trading desk of a brokerage house. Now, the Chicago Mercantile Exchange (CME) and other exchanges have electronic order entry systems that allow anyone with a laptop, a trading account, and internet access to trade virtually around the globe, around the clock.

The CME's electronic system is the Globex. The Chicago Board of Trade, or CBOT, also has an electronic trading system called the a/c/e. These electronic trading systems can be accessed through on-line brokerage accounts via computer. On weekday afternoons, the S&P Futures open for Globex trading at 3:30 P.M. The Dow Futures night session opens at 7:15 P.M. Night trading is very different from trading during the day session. There is far less volume and everything moves slowly. I have placed orders, gone to dinner, returned, and my positions were basically unchanged. If trading at night, be prepared to wait on the market.

As the evening wears on, markets around the globe get going. Shortly after the sun rises in the east, Asia opens for business and dominates the global scene. For example, at 6:00 P.M., the Nikkei opens in Tokyo. A short time later, the Hang Seng market opens in Hong Kong. Active Asian markets have the ability to exert some degree of influence on U.S. markets. Therefore, if the Asian markets are down, you might want to think twice before going long on the S&P or the Dow. Conversely, if Eastern markets are showing a lot of strength, you probably want to look to the long side of U.S. markets, or at least exercise caution before going short.

The DAX, a German Futures contract, opens at 2:00 A.M. and the CAC, the French market, the FTSE, the London market, and the Swiss markets also open around this time. Because Germany has the largest economy in Europe, it carries a big stick. The DAX is often a major market mover in the early hours of Globex trading. If the DAX is extremely strong, expect the Dow and the S&P to gain strength. When you see that same upward momentum in Asia, Europe, and the United States, there is confirmation that the markets have a bullish tone. Divergence among these markets tells you to stay out. If domestic and foreign markets are all trending lower, it is a sign of weakness and you may be able to take advantage of it with a sell. To improve your trading, get a clear view of global markets and use that knowledge.

When the European markets open, the Asian markets are approaching closing time. Therefore, the European markets (especially the DAX) take the spotlight from Asia and become the world's most active trading centers.

Major financial markets in the United States open between 8:00 A.M. and 9:00 A.M. The S&P Futures opens at 8:30 A.M. Once these markets begin trading, a lot of global attention transfers to our shores. As morning trading in the United States progresses, foreign markets have less and less influence on the day's activities. The DAX Futures ends electronic trading at 1:00 P.M. and the United States again dominates trading until the Asian markets open in the early evening hours. Then, the cycle begins again with the most active global trading beginning in Asia, moving to Europe, and finally on to the United States. It follows the path of the sun as it moves from east to west.

In trading, ignorance is not bliss. Ignorance generally translates into an empty account and a lot of heartbreak. You may be trading U.S. markets, but it pays to be aware of what is happening in the other major financial centers around the globe. Some United States companies are listed on foreign exchanges. The stock prices of these big international companies reflect how the world values United States stocks and how they interpret the world financial scene. It really is a small world, especially with the advances of technology. If there is a major problem in Asia or Europe, it will be reflected in domestic markets. Likewise, if there is a major problem in the United States, do not expect the problem to be isolated to this side of the pond. Expect the problem to be reflected quickly on foreign markets, just as it was in 1987. The larger the problem, the bigger the global impact will be. Therefore, to improve your trading and get a clear view, I highly recommend that you use a 24-hour trading clock and stay generally abreast of how foreign indices, stocks, and exchanges are doing.

Using a 24-hour trading clock gives me an edge and helps me to be a better, more informed trader. It also opens new trading avenues for me, such as allowing me to trade the DAX Futures Index.

Exercise Caution when Trading the Night Market

The night market is very different from the day market. As you can imagine, there are far fewer players. Therefore, I feel compelled to give you a few words of warning. First, observe and study the market before you trade it. Note the way it moves and the times that are most active. One of those active times is 2:00 A.M., when the DAX opens. The energy of the Germans seems to be contagious and U.S. markets generally respond with some increased movement.

Another point that I want to make is that even though I trade the night market, I do not carry my trades over from the day. Let me explain. The day trading session ends in the afternoon. The S&P Futures close at 3:15 P.M. and the Dow closes at 4:00 P.M. If you do not exit the market at that time, you are deemed to be holding your positions overnight and the clearing houses require a much greater margin requirement for doing so. For example, it is possible to trade an e-mini S&P contract for a margin requirement of only $1,000.00. That is, if you do not carry your position over from the day session into the night session. However, if you hold that contract overnight, the margin requirement increases to $4,500.00. That is quite a difference! If you want to trade in the evenings without paying higher margins, you must exit the market when it closes at 3:15 P.M. or so and reenter after the night market opens. The S&P Futures reopens at 3:30 P.M. and the Dow Futures reopens at 7:15 P.M. Therefore, if you want to be in the market, just get out at 3:15 P.M. and reenter at 3:30 P.M. (For the S&P, that is, other indices or exchanges may have other hours.). Once you reenter, you can hold those positions until the close of the day sessions on the following day.

When people talk about the risk of day trading, I always think about these exchange rules. The exchanges are the biggest handicappers in the world. They require substantially more risk dollars for those who are trading futures and holding them overnight with a buy and hold strategy than they do for those using a day trading strategy. Just think about that!

Again, be careful if you plan to trade after the day session ends. I enjoy trading at night, but I have played these games since their inception and I know a lot of maneuvers and tricks. If you do not, the times can be extremely treacherous. Why do you think that Dracula creeps about at night? He is sucking the blood out of unsuspecting people. Some expert night traders try to do the same to the less informed traders. Wall Street acknowledges the inherent dangers and expresses them by increasing the required margins.

Just be sure that if you trade at night that you prepare for it. Don't let some market Dracula suck your account dry!

THE TIME OF YEAR IS ALSO IMPORTANT

In addition to using the time of day and the 24-hour trading clock, I also use the time of year to help me increase my profits. Certain times during the year are more important than others. When the market opens on January 1, the bulls and the bears begin their battle. The year is new and each side has 365 days to impose its bias on the market. The past year's market trend may continue, or it may end and a new trend may begin. For example, take 2005. The prior year ended on an up-note. During the last couple of months of 2004, the S&P Futures rose by about a hundred points. That is a pretty big move.

Seeing the big gains of December 2004, a novice might think that a rally in 2005 was assured. The opening price for 2005 on the S&P Futures was 1213.50. But, as the New Year began, there was uncertainty. Would the rally continue or would the market retrace? At least in January, the rally did not continue. The bears came out in force and by the end of the month, the S&P was trading about 50 points lower than the yearly open. Will the market decline in 2005 and return to 2004 average prices? No one knows. I do know, however, that throughout the year, the opening price of 1213.50 on the S&P futures will be very important. If the bulls are able to get the market above it, look for a rally.

I consider the yearly opening price of a market to be the single most important pivot number for that market during the entire year. In the early days of January 2005, it was clear that there was a war raging between the bulls and the bears. At the time of this writing, it is still not known who will win the battle of 2005. If you only remember one number for the whole year, remember the opening price of the market(s) you trade. Use that number wisely; it should allow you to put some additional money in the bank.

Let's look at another example. In 2004, the S&P Futures opening price was 1111.00 (Figure 2.1). Throughout the year, I kept my eye on that number. If the market fell to it and broke below it, I knew that the bears were strong and I prepared for a sell off. If the market moved above it, I started looking long. In November, as it approached 1111.00, I watched carefully to see if the bulls could push higher. I knew that if they broke the year's opening price, the market would move up and test higher prices. With the Christmas holidays approaching, the 1111.00 price was broken and there was no turning back. The S&P Futures did not look back until January 1, 2005, when the market reversed for a few weeks. Even with the reversal, it was far above 1111.00.

Notice in Figure 2.1 the market's reaction to the 1111.00 price. Also note the big move at the end of 2004. Once the bulls got the market above its yearly opening price, the holiday spirit jumped in and pressed the market higher. By the time merrymakers welcomed in the New Year, the S&P Futures had made a gain of over 100 points.

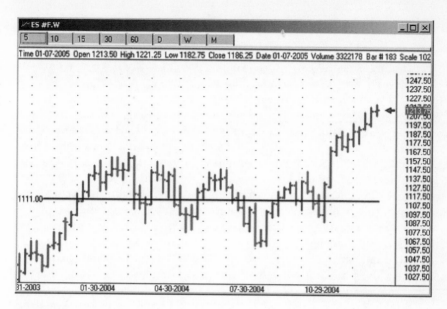

FIGURE 2.1   Note the S&P Futures and the significance of the yearly opening.
Source: www.dtitrader.com

The opening bell on January 2 of each and every year is the start of the trading game. This date is the single most important day in the market during the entire year. *Write it down!*

Holidays and Other Dates Are Significant

New Year's Day is not the only important date to watch. There are a number of other holidays that tend to affect the global markets. I rarely experience an emotional high on April 15, but the markets tend to respect this date. If the markets have been trending prior to tax day in the United States, look for the trend to accelerate. Or, the markets may reverse after this date. It is one of those watershed days when the markets seem to reconsider the direction that they are taking. After reconsideration, the trend may be reaffirmed and revved up or reevaluated and reversed. Other similar dates include Memorial Day, July 4, Labor Day, Thanksgiving, and Christmas.

I love the Christmas season. December is historically a fantastic trading month for me. The markets tend to be bullish and they move. I make a lot of money in December as the holiday cheer spreads on Wall Street. Exercise caution when taking a bearish stance in late November and December. There will be down days, but generally even Wall Street traders get overtaken by the holiday season.

Time Is Also a Healer—It Clears the Mind

A final way that I use time is to clear my mind. Sometimes we all get in a rut. Our trading is just not working. We lose on Monday and we lose more on Tuesday. By Friday, we wish we had not traded at all during the week. If you find yourself in a losing streak, quit. Stop trading for a while. Take a break. Clear your mind.

One of my students was experiencing an awful losing streak. It had become so bad that when she placed a trade, she assumed she would lose. Her lack of confidence and her fear made her expectation a reality. She was part of a class of about twenty students. Other students in the class made some of the same trades she made, but executed them differently. For example, they entered the trade sooner or held it longer and they made money. She, on the other, hesitated and entered trades late or took tiny profits and exited her positions too early. She was sabotaging herself. I tried to tell her this, but she would not listen. I told her that she needed to take a short break from trading and clear her mind. I encouraged her to paper trade or do some trade simulations until she got her confidence back.

She responded negatively, "I can't quit. I have to make money this month because I have some bills I want to pay." Stubbornly she rejected my advice and kept trading. Soon, she was not trading at all because her account was empty.

Time can help break a losing streak by getting you out of the market, enabling you to identify and correct your errors. If nothing else, it stops the losing until you can readjust to the market and improve your strategy.

When you take a break, use the time off to evaluate your trading. What did you do wrong? Was it timing? Did you misread the indicators? Did fear or greed destroy your trading strategy? Is the market too jittery or too unpredictable for some reason? How can you improve?

After your mind has cleared and you have considered your strengths and your weaknesses, get back into the trading game. Start slowly. Paper trade or trade simulations only. When you begin trading your actual account, take a couple of small positions. If they are profitable, slowly increase your trading until it is back to full speed. Let your confidence rebuild before you attempt to take on a large position.

Use Time as a Trading Element, but Do Not Give Trading Your Life

You need to use a 24-hour trading clock, but that does not mean that you should sit before your computer 24-hours a day and trade. RoadMap software records 24-hour market data for me. I can sleep well knowing that the information will be waiting for me when I get up. There are other ways to track and record data. Find one. The best thing you can do for yourself is seek out, test, and incorporate trading tools that simplify your trading career.

Keep up with the markets, but remember to trade only when you have a high probability of making money. When the market is not moving or when you cannot determine its direction, get away. Play golf, watch television, clean the house, do whatever you need or want to do.

If you carefully select the times when you trade, you will be able to make more money and you will be able to better enjoy your life.

REVIEW

Golf is my favorite sport. For decades, I have taken lessons and worked to improve my game. Years ago, Ron Gring, my instructor, told me that golf was a game of opposites. For example, if you want to drive the ball a great distance, you can't focus on the hole that awaits you yards and yards away; instead, you must focus on the small ball that is inches from your feet. In order to get your ball to travel a far distance, you must come to a stop. You must execute a deliberate swing with concentration and calculated force. If you focus on the power behind your swing; you may well get a choppy swing that misses the ball altogether or barely grazes it and leaves you in the dust.

In that way, trading is like golf. In order to make more money, you need to trade less, but with deliberation. The inexperienced trader often thinks that he or she needs to trade all of the time; that is not true. A trader who trades too much will, very likely, waste both time and money.

Time is a very significant element in trading. You want to trade when there is the greatest volatility and liquidity because that is when you can be profitable. If you trade during the times that I have designated as my Trade Zones, these essential elements will generally be present. Also, if you limit your trading to these times, you enhance your probability of success in another way; you limit the likelihood that you will over trade. Over trading is a sure path to depleting your account.

Paying attention to global time and using a 24-hour trading clock is also very important. In this age of technology and enhanced communication, activities around the globe affect markets. Knowing how Asia and Europe are trading is very important to your market analysis. It can improve your trading by informing you of the world's view of the marketplace.

Timing is also important when looking at global holidays and events. Take note of the New Year's open, April 15, Memorial Day, Labor Day, Thanksgiving, and Christmas. Remember that these dates may signal a market shift or acceleration. Note how the market trades on these dates and adjust your trading accordingly.

Finally, if you are experiencing some problems with your trading, take a break. Stop playing the game for a while. Take time off to rejuvenate yourself and reassess your trading. Relax and evaluate. Identify errors and make a plan for correction. By using all the aspects of time effectively, your trading should improve.

 LESSONS LEARNED

- Patience pays.
- Trade during the times of greatest liquidity and volatility.
- Use a 24-hour trading clock.
- Do not overtrade.
- Remember the yearly opening price of the markets that you plan to trade and use that number as a major pivot throughout the year.

CHAPTER 3

Trading Is a Numbers Game

O n Tuesday, March 30, 1999, the Dow broke 10,000 points. For years, market watchers had anxiously awaited this momentous event. Conventional Wall Street wisdom predicted that once the number was hit, such a strong force of resistance would be exerted that there would be a major market reversal. Due to this belief, every time the market approached the 10,000 mark, sellers stepped in and pushed it down. Finally, after a number of approaches, the big 10,000 was reached and surpassed. Due to the significance of 10,000, it took a long time.

Every index, stock, and commodity has certain numbers that are recognized as more important than others, and I refer to them as key numbers. I do not know why this is true, but I am certain that it is. When the particular market approaches or hits these key numbers, they serve as points of support or resistance and are, therefore, pivotal numbers in the market. Professionals are aware of key numbers and their significance and they use them to make money. If you want to be a successful trader, you must also learn to use key numbers to your advantage. Like time, key numbers are another important element of my trading strategy.

USING KEY NUMBERS IS NOT NEW

Since the birth of the stock market, there have been many outstanding traders. I enjoy reading about their lives and their trading methods. Few of them have captured my imagination and my respect as much as Jesse

Livermore, the Great Bear of Wall Street. Throughout this book I refer to Livermore often because I identify with his trading style and I respect his rags-to-riches story. Richard Smitten tells the interesting story of Livermore's life in the book, *The Amazing Life of Jesse Livermore*, published by Traders Press. At the age of 14, Livermore began his journey from humble beginnings to great wealth. With a few dollars in his pocket, he left his hometown and set out for Boston. As soon as he arrived, he jumped from the wagon transporting him and walked into the Paine Webber office. He sought a position and was immediately hired as a chalkboard boy. The duties of a chalkboard boy were not complex, but they required focus and accuracy. Numbers were called from a ticker tape and Jesse had to correctly record the numbers on a blackboard in the front of the room for brokers and clients to read.

As Livermore recorded the stock prices, he began to see certain numbers repeat over and over again and he saw the patterns formed by these repetitions. Livermore did not have the advantages of technology that we have today. No computer tracked and recorded his data or generated charts for him to study. Livermore jotted down the numbers in a numerical diary. He kept the diary in his pocket and studied it as frequently as possible. The significance of the repeating patterns impressed him and it was not long before he was using the information to make money by trading stocks. Once he identified a pattern, he was able to use that pattern effectively. If you want to succeed at the game, like Livermore, you have to study the numbers and find and use the patterns. Identifying key numbers will help you to do that.

On October 24, 1907, Livermore was 30 years old and he made his first million-dollar trade. That is right, on one trade he made a million dollars and according to Smitten, he made it in one day. A million dollar trade is huge today; think of how big it was in 1907.

Studying key numbers may not get you a million dollars in a day or a lifetime, but I guarantee you that if you learn the key numbers of the market you are trading and you use those numbers wisely, your trading will improve. Education is the secret.

WHAT ARE KEY NUMBERS AND HOW ARE THEY ESTABLISHED

What is a key number? A key number is a price that the market respects for some reason. It is a point at which the market has a tendency to exert some level of support or resistance. A line is often drawn in the sand at this point and the bulls or the bears dare the other to cross it. The market honors these numbers. Some key numbers are very strong; whereas others are much weaker. Key numbers are established in different ways. Some key numbers are historically important. That is, over time, these numbers have established themselves in the market and the market tends to hold them in high regard. Other numbers are important because they have exhibited strength and significance in recent trading. As noted previously, all key numbers are not created equally. Some key numbers are major pivotal numbers, like the 10,000 was for the Dow in 1999. Other key numbers are minor pivots and may hold support or resistance only briefly. To be a good trader you must know the numbers that the market respects. Believe me, the big boys know the numbers and if you do not, you will likely get clobbered because you will have a habit of buying the highs and selling the lows. Use key numbers to avoid this mistake.

Stocks Respect Key Numbers

Not only are there key numbers on exchanges and indices, but equities also respect key numbers. Through the school of hard knocks, I learned that 100.00 is a key number for most equities. If a stock breaks 100.00, it is likely to go to 110.00. I remember becoming aware of this fact when I was trading Merrill Lynch stock. I was short the stock and it broke 100.00. I held tight and waited for the price action to reverse. However, I watched in dismay and shock as the stock headed for 110.00, taking my money with it. Since that time, I have understood the power of 100.00 in the equities market and I have repeatedly used that knowledge to make money. If IBM, Microsoft, eBay, or any other stock that I am trading breaks 100.00, I will not be short. I will be a buyer and I will have my ultimate profit target set at or near 110.00. Or, I will be on the sidelines, but I will not be short (Figure 3.1).

If you are trading a particular stock, study it and determine the pivotal numbers that are key for that stock. At what points have support and resistance been established? Be sure to get the yearly open for the stock and the historical highs and lows. Study trading patterns during certain times of day and of the year to determine the points where support and resistance will likely be strongest. This will help you see the rhythm of the market and get in step with it. Do not make the mistake of underestimating the power of key numbers.

Key Numbers in Commodities

Key numbers are also critical in the commodity markets. Consider crude oil. Fifty dollars a barrel was said to be a huge number for crude. Like the 10,000 level on the Dow, analysts carefully watched the $50.00 per barrel price. That number was actually hit and surpassed in 2004, and crude oil rose to $56.00 per barrel. In 2005, oil soared even higher. Once a major point of support or resistance is broken, the market is free to move to the next key number (Figure 3.2).

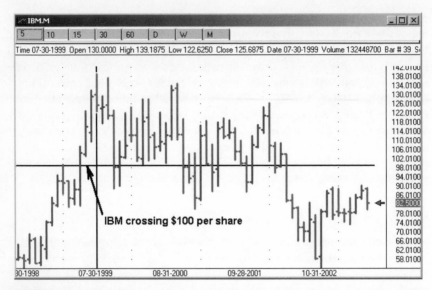

FIGURE 3.1 Note what happened to IBM when the price crossed $100.00 a share.
Source: www.dtitrader.com

FIGURE 3.2 Note the market's response when oil crossed the $50.00 per barrel price.
Source: www.dtitrader.com

A friend of mine, Big E, was short oil in 2004. Needless to say, when oil surpassed the $50.00 a barrel price, he was really hurting. In 2005, Big E reversed his strategy. He skillfully used the $50.00 price as a pivot number and bought the market. In June 2005, as oil hit $58.00, Big E was enjoying his profitable repositioning. Knowing key numbers pays in every market.

Before trading a commodity, observe it for a while. Just like stocks, observe patterns over time. Look at some daily charts and determine the places where you will likely encounter resistance. Then use these points to help you to make money.

Sometimes commodities are affected by external factors and the prices basically go wild. The war in Iraq stressed the oil market and led to the huge price increase in 2004 and 2005. At other times, shortages, gluts, or environmental factors will cause huge swings in other commodities. Therefore, if you are trading commodities, there are many factors to consider. However, key numbers are certainly one of the important things to research before entering the commodities markets.

Key Numbers Are Huge in the Futures Markets

All markets have key numbers that hold respect, including the futures indices. Years ago, I realized that the big S&P Futures contract likes to move in 0.50 increments. For example, if the price of 1167.00 is hit, there is an increased chance that 1167.50 or 1166.50 will also be hit. I use this knowledge to help me to determine optimum protective stop placement. Say, for example, that I am long the S&P Futures from 1167.00. I need to determine the best spot for my protective stop. I do not want it too close and I do not want it too far away from where the market is trading. Because I have studied key numbers, I know that 1165.00 is historically a key number on this index. With my added knowledge that the big S&P likes to move in 0.50 increments, I am better able to select my protective stop placement. Therefore, I put my protective stop at the 1164.40. (I want to get below 1165.00 by the 0.50 and then give the market one more tick so that if the index drops to the 1165.50 number, then reverses back up, I will be safe.)

Look at another example: If I am short the big S&P Futures from 1167.00, I know that the next key number where resistance will be exerted is 1169.00. I know this because nine's are important numbers in this market. Again, in addition to knowing that the 1169.00 is a key number, I know that this particular market likes to move in increments of 0.50. Therefore, I place my protective stop at 1169.00 and add the 0.50 that the market is likely to hit. I give the market at least one more tick for good measure and place my protective stop at 1169.60.

This knowledge of trading patterns and key numbers has paid me for years. Your trading will benefit too if you know and use key numbers.

HOW I USE KEY NUMBERS TO ANALYZE THE MARKET

Another way that I use key numbers is to form a big picture of the market. Traders need both a big picture or long-term understanding of the market and also a smaller or a short-term picture. Key numbers help me to accomplish this objective and form a framework for my analysis. With my analysis, I start with the big view and incrementally move down to the smaller frame and then to the trade at hand.

Here is the method I follow. As stated in Chapter 2, when each year begins, I record the opening price for every stock, index, commodity, and other trading vehicle that I think I may want to trade during the course of the year. In 2005, I recorded the opening price for the S&P Futures (1213.50), the Dow Futures (10,781), the Nasdaq Futures (1628.00), the DAX Futures (4284.00), and some stocks that I thought I might trade, for example eBay (EBAY), Research in Motion Limited (RIMM), and Exxon Mobil (XOM), just to name a few.

This yearly opening price is the first big pivot number that I etch in my mind. Throughout the entire year, if the market trades above it, I consider the big picture more bullish. If the market trades below it, I consider the market to have a somewhat bearish tendency. How bullish or how bearish the market is depends on how far above or below that opening price it is trading.

After I know the yearly open, I follow the consecutive weekly opens. As each week of January begins, I write down that weekly opening price and I compare it to both the yearly opening price and to the opening prices of the weeks before. Is the market trading above or below these previous opens? I record the weekly opens and I make a trend line of these prices. This trend line keeps me focused on the big picture.

As the year progresses, on the first day of each month, I follow this same procedure; I record the month's opening price. With each new week, I record the weekly opens and I plot them on my trend line. If the opening monthly price of the S&P Futures is greater in May than it was in April, I look more to the bullish side. If several consecutive months exhibit this bullish tendency, I will only short the market with great care. I, of course, also consider the monthly opens in comparison to the yearly open. By focusing on the market from month to month and week to week, I keep the big picture in mind and I gain an understanding of the overall structure of the market. You may want to refer to Chapter 4 and the examples of the trend lines for early 2005. They are depicted in Figures 4.2 through 4.5.

Why is this information important? Some years back, in evaluating the market, I discovered what I believed to be an essential part of its code. A lot of traders pay attention to market closing prices and ignore the opens. I reversed the order and I think the big secret is in the opening prices.

Even when we are experiencing a strong bullish period, there will be times when the market will retrace and consolidate. Or, during doom and gloom times when the bears are trouncing the bulls, there will be some attempts to rally. If you are not aware of the underlying sentiment of the market, you may be tempted to sell or buy at just the wrong time. Watching market openings helps me detect that underlying market sentiment.

The opening price for the first day of the year for 2005 was the high of the month of January. As the months passed, I always remembered the opening price and used it to evaluate the market. At the time of this writing, it is May, 2005. As I look back I realize that by having a big picture view, I saved myself from mistakes that a lot of folks made. In the face of the big rally we had in 2004, a huge percentage of investors (maybe as many as 95 percent) probably thought the rally would continue in early 2005. But, my big picture approach helped me to understand the gyrations of the market.

Another example is Fed Day in May of 2005. On May 3, 2005, when the Fed made their announcement at 1:15 P.M., I was well aware of the fact that on the S&P Futures Index, we were trading below the daily opening of 1164.00. Therefore, I was looking to short the market. I did so and my students and I had a nice ten-minute run to 1157.00. While everyone else was tying to figure out Mr. Greenspan, we were using our method and making money.

With a big picture framework in your head, you will be better prepared to properly analyze the market's behavior and respond appropriately. You will know how the numbers fit together and their significance. This will save you money.

Use This Approach with Options, Too

I use a variation of this approach with options. On expiration date, look at the closing price for underling stock covered by the option. Is that price above or below the yearly opening price for that stock? If it is above the opening price, look to the long side. In late 2004, I used this strategy very successfully with Apple. I noticed that the monthly closing price was above the yearly opening price and I bought the stock and stock options at $60.00. I had a fantastic run as the price soared from $30.00 to $40.00 (Figure 3.3).

Move from the Big Picture to the Little Picture

From the monthly and weekly opens, I move to the daily numbers. My method begins with a wide screen and focuses upon smaller and smaller

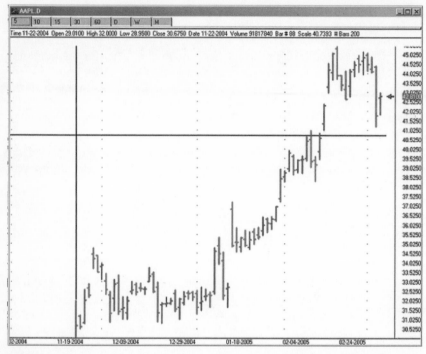

FIGURE 3.3   Note the big move as Apple's price soars from $30.00 to $40.00.
Source: www.dtitrader.com

time frames and numbers until I see the current market. Every day, I want
to know the daily opens and the daily closes. What was the daily trend on
Monday, on Tuesday, etc.? Next, I look within each day at some additional
numbers that I consider noteworthy. First, I want the high and the low price
for the previous day's trading. Then, I want the high and the low for the
Globex (the previous night market). The highs and the lows of the markets
are important because they tell me where the market has recently established support and resistance. I also want the previous day's 12:30 P.M.
number, the 6:00 A.M. DAX number, and the 3:30 A.M. number for the S&P
Futures. Throughout my trading day, I consider these important numbers
and I record them before the day's trading begins. I refer to these numbers
and use them as a gauge to evaluate the activity of the market as the day's
trading progresses. I want to know if we are trading above or below yesterday's high, or above or below yesterday's 12:30 P.M. number. With these
numbers, I am able to plot market direction and identify trends. Using so
many numbers might seem confusing, but if you plot them out on a piece of
graph paper, you will see the code.

At 12:30 P.M., the Market Hits the Reset Button

As stated previously, the 12:30 P.M. number is a big pivot number for me. By observation over a good deal of time, I realized the significance of this number. Every day, after traders return from lunch, they seem to survey the market with a fresh look and the market tends to refresh and reset itself at this time. That does not mean that there will always be a retracement, but it does mean that this time is a watershed in daily trading when markets, exchanges, and indices may retrace, reverse, or accelerate a trend that has been established during the day. I consider the 12:30 P.M. trading price to be a very important number. This number will be significant to the market until a new number is formed at 12:30 P.M. the next day.

The 6:00 A.M. DAX Futures number holds the same importance in the German market as does the 12:30 P.M. United States number. At 6:00 A.M. Central Time in the United States, the DAX market is going through the same general activities that U.S. markets are going through at 12:30 P.M. This is a time when the DAX market is reevaluating and may reverse or accelerate an existing move. Therefore, the DAX 6:00 A.M. trading price is also very important to me.

I consider one other number important: I record and note the 3:30 A.M. number on the S&P Futures. I believe that this number is significant because it reflects how European traders view U.S. markets during some of their most active trading. Refer to the daily key numbers that I record and watch. I strongly suggest that you record the applicable key numbers for the investment vehicle that you are trading.

> **Daily key numbers for the S&P Futures**
>
> Yesterday's High
>
> Yesterday's Low
>
> Globex High
>
> Globex Low
>
> 12:30 P.M. price
>
> 3:30 A.M. price
>
> 6:00 A.M. DAX Futures price
>
> Remember that all times are Central

Narrow the Focus Again

In addition to the key numbers, I also use 30-minute bar charts to focus in on the moment. Over my nearly 30 years of trading, I have tried using

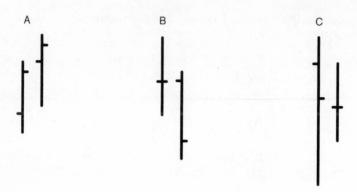

FIGURE 3.4 Figure A represents an up-trend. Figure B represents down-trend. Figure C represent no trend because the second bar is inside the first one.
Source: www.dtitrader.com

all sorts of methods and various charting techniques. However, for me, the most useful chart is one that records trading for 30-minute time frames. The key numbers on the chart are the highs and the lows of each 30-minute bar. Figure 3.4 is an illustration of the only charts that I use on a daily basis. These bars each represent 30-minute trading on the S&P Futures index. The charts are incredibly simple and clear and most of the time these rather elementary charts, combined with other aspects of my method, keep me on the right side of the market.

In example A, the second bar has higher highs and higher lows than the first bar. For the short term, the market is indicating a bullish move. In example B, the second bar has lower highs and lower lows and is, of course, indicating a bearish trend for the immediate time frame shown. Example C shows no trend. The second bar is contained inside the first bar. It is impossible to determine whether or not the market wants to go up or down. This is a clear signal to sit on your hands and keep them away from your mouse. Trading with this type of charting pattern is like flipping a coin or sitting down at a slot machine. You cannot possibly use this chart for any reason except to stay out of the market.

As traders, we sometimes feel that we have to trade. We have been watching the market for hours and if we do not trade we feel that we have wasted our time. However, correctly deciding to stay out of a bad market is a very important decision and is far better than taking a bad trade and losing money. Why foolishly enter the market and live to regret it? Remember that money you lose today is money you have to make tomorrow.

During the day's trading session, the most important 30-minute bars are the bars formed between 8:30 A.M. and 9:00 A.M. and between 12:30 P.M. and

1:00 P.M. I call these bars reference bars because I refer to them to gauge the market during the applicable trade zones. I note the highs and the lows of these bars to determine whether the market is, at the immediate time, being bullish or bearish.

When I analyze the market, I start with the big picture and move down to smaller frames until I zero in on the immediate market. By this method of moving from the big or more distant trading to the near or immediate trading, I am able to gain a clearer focus and, I believe, improve my chances of success. Many times, because I understand the big picture, I can stay on the right side of things and make money. It also helps me successfully identify false market moves and prevent losses.

HISTORICAL KEY NUMBERS

In every market there are some numbers that are historically significant. When you trade an index you should learn its key numbers. For example, take the Dow Futures. The historical key numbers on the Dow Futures are easy to remember because they are each quarter and five points on either side of the quarter. That is, 00, 25, 50, and 75 and five points on either side of these numbers. The 50 and the 00 are major pivot numbers and the 25 and the 75 are minor pivot numbers.

Watch the Dow Futures trade. If the Dow is trading at 10,482, the next historical point of major resistance will likely be 10,500. Once 10,500 is clearly broken, the next point of minor historical resistance will be 10,525. If 10,525 is broken, expect the index to attempt to challenge 10,550. Of course, these historical numbers are not the only key numbers that are significant on the Dow. As noted in the previous sections, there are other numbers that exert points of support and resistance as the market trades every day. You need to be aware of these numbers too.

Historically key numbers on the Dow Futures Index

00	25	50	75

Expect the market to exert major support or resistance at the 50 and 00 levels and minor support or resistance at the 25 and 75 levels. For example, 10,400, 10,500 and 10,600 and 10,450, 10,550 and 10,650 are numbers that will exert major influence and 10,425 and 10,475, 10,525 and 10,575 will exert minor resistance or support.

HISTORICAL KEY NUMBERS ON THE S&P FUTURES

Now, let's take a look at the S&P Futures Index. There is a relatively long list of historical key numbers on this index. Like the Dow, expect 00 to be important. For example 1100.00, 1200.00, and 1300.00 will be strong. In addition, two, seven, and nine may also be key numbers. (That means that 902.00, or 1152, or any number ending in 2, 7, or 9 may be important.) Observe the S&P for yourself and watch it trade. Notice that when 1172.00, or 1182.00, or 1202.00, and so forth are hit, these numbers tend to be pivotal points. Likewise, expect 1177.00, 1277.00, and 1377.00 to be important numbers.

There are many other historically important numbers on the S&P Futures Index. Some of them are listed in Figure 3.6. Many of my students copy this list and tape it on or near their computers for easy, quick reference. They believe that recognizing and using these numbers positively impacts their trading.

When you are using historical key numbers, remember that you must put them in the context of the current market. Look at them relative to where the market is trading and note how the market has responded to them recently. For example, there will be times when a number will be very strong and for a week or so, every time that the number is hit, the market will either exert support or resistance. By monitoring the market, you will get an idea of the strength of some of these numbers.

```
          Some historically important numbers
                on the S&P Futures Index

          02        32        52        75
          06        35        55        77
          09        37        57–58     81
          12        42        63–64     84
          15        45        69        87
          27        47        72        92
                    50                  98
```

HOW I USE KEY NUMBERS TO TRADE

I Use Key Numbers to Enter the Market

Because key numbers are points of support and resistance in the market, I use them in several ways. First, if I am looking for a point to buy or sell the market, I certainly do not want to buy the market just before a point of major resistance. I want to wait for the market to break above that resistance before buying. Every trader has had the experience of buying the daily, weekly, or monthly high, only to have the market reverse and go down. Then, an anticipated profit quickly becomes a loss. Likewise, we have all sold at a support level. In my dark years I seemed to have a special knack for buying the highs and selling the lows. Obviously, you do not want to sell if you are sitting on a level of key support. Wait for support to be broken before entering the market to the short side.

I Use Key Numbers to Set Profit Targets

I also use key numbers to establish profit targets. If I buy the S&P at 1209.00 and the yearly open was 1213.50, I know that the market will show a great deal of resistance at that yearly opening price. Therefore, I want to take some of my profits and lighten my position before hitting this known level of major resistance. If a number is very strong, the market may have to try to break it a number of times before it succeeds. After resistance is broken, then I may want to enter the market again or add to an existing position. At that point, the old resistance level becomes new support and I look for the next level of resistance to take additional profits. The same holds true if support levels are broken. I look for the next support level for profit taking.

If you do not take at least some of your profits at support and resistance levels, you may live to regret it. I always like to get paid. I do not want to hold my positions too long. If you get greedy the market may move against you. Remember, you are trading to make money.

I Use Key Numbers for Protective Stop Placement

Finally, I use key numbers to set protective stops. If you want to protect your capital, never trade without a protective stop. One of the things I drive into the heads of everyone I am teaching is that you cannot trade without a stop. Doing so is just plain foolish.

As all experienced traders know, stop placement is a tricky business. For effective stop placement, you need to be aware of and respect key numbers. When I am looking for a good spot to place my protective stop, I identify the next key number. I place the stop on the opposite side of that number. Review the example of that method in the previous section on key numbers in the S&P Futures Index. Believe me when I tell you that these pages on key numbers are very important. You need to read them again and again until you really understand it. This concept is too important to miss.

REVIEW

Almost every stock, index, exchange, and commodity respects some numbers more than others. These key numbers are pivotal points where support and resistance are established. By learning the key numbers, you can select optimum points of entry, set profit targets, and determine proper protective stop placement. Many traders know and use key numbers. Key numbers are the points where these traders draw the line in the sand and dare the market to cross.

Observation is the best way to learn key numbers. Watch a stock or an index trade for awhile and identify the pivotal points. Study weekly and daily charts and notice the points at which prices shift. Having a good working knowledge of key numbers will provide you with moneymaking opportunities. I cannot imagine trading without using key numbers. I would be lost. Key numbers are my compass; they lead me through the market maze.

 LESSONS LEARNED

- Use key numbers to get the big picture.
- Record yearly opening prices and remember them.
- Start with the yearly open and use monthly and weekly opening prices to form a trend line. This will let you know whether the market has a long-term bias. If so, it will help you identify the bias.
- Every market has certain numbers that hold significance in that market. Learn these numbers and use them.
- Use key numbers to determine points of entry, exit, and to establish profit targets.

CHAPTER 4

Read the Tape

W hen I landed my first job in the financial services industry, my employers sent me to New York, one of the most exciting cities in the world, for training. For a small town southern boy, it was an eye-opening experience. One of the most fascinating, and certainly the liveliest, places I visited was Wall Street. The floor of the New York Stock Exchange is always jumping. People move around faster than a hive of worker bees. Everyone is yelling and shouting. On the surface it looks like total chaos, but you soon learn that it is an orderly chaos. All of the players have a clear understanding of how the game is played and they understand their role in it. During the course of my training, I received many hours of instruction on corporate research. I learned the traditional methods used to rate and select various stocks and investments. A lot of my time was spent on learning the intricacies of technical analysis. I was a good student and studied hard. I had a desire to learn about the markets because I enjoyed investing. When I left the big city, I admit that I truly believed that I knew something and I was proud of it. Little did I know the extent of my ignorance!

Immediately upon my return to Oklahoma City and the local brokerage office, I reported for duty. One of my fellow brokers, Chappy, had been working in the financial management field for almost 30 years. I saw him busy at work and stepped over to speak to him. On the corner of his desk was an enormous pile of paperwork. A voluminous stack of research detailing just about anything anyone would want to know about dozens and dozens of companies and their stocks.

I struck up a conversation with Chappy, just small talk. I wanted him to know how much I knew. After a few minutes, he smiled at me and said, "See all of this research. These papers contain millions of dollars worth of analytical studies. In this pile of papers are ratios, charts, and all sorts of information, but all of that stuff really doesn't matter." Then, he took his arm and shoved that huge stack of paper right off the desk and right into the trash. "See that," he pointed to the tickertape running across one wall of the office. "That, my friend, is all that matters. If you want to make money on Wall Street, learn to read that tape."

Today, after I have been investing and trading for almost 30 years, I agree with Chappy. If you want to be a successful trader, you have to learn to read the tape. Reading the tape is much more than just looking at a number running across a bar. Reading the tape means understanding the significance of the numbers as they move and understanding them in relation to other numbers and other data, including time. It is a skill that is learned with much effort.

SOMETIMES, THERE IS TOO MUCH OF A GOOD THING

In my office I have an old tape reader. It is a nice conversation piece. With the tiny band of paper, it looks almost like a small cash register receipt. It is incredible to think that years ago that simple machine was the way traders received market data. In fact, that original tape reader, slow and awkward as it must have been, was actually superior to previous methods (Figure 4.1).

I have heard stories about early days when flagmen actually transmitted data from Wall Street to Philadelphia. These men stood on high ground and communicated stock prices by the movements of their flags. Each flagman received data from the man before him, and he, in turn, sent the information on down the line to the next flagman. Wow! In the age of information, that seems almost unbelievable. I wonder how accurate those transmissions were?

Today, with a computer, an internet connection, and a data feed source that transmits real time quotes, we can get more information than we want. We can gather all sorts of numbers and charts and watch dozens of indicators. In fact, frequently, there is so much data that it is difficult to determine what is useful and what is garbage. If you get too much data it is confusing and impossible to know what to do. Later in this chapter, I explain the indicators I use and how I interpret them. As you trade, you will gather the indicators that you find to be the most reliable. Just do not try to get too much information because it will confuse you. At least today we do not suffer from a lack of information (Figure 4.2).

FIGURE 4.1   Stock prices were transmitted via a small tape reader.
Source: www.dtitrader.com

Roadmap Page: Default Day							_ □ ×
10:45:46	ES M5	NQ M5	YM M5	TTICK	AX M5-DT	AAPL	EBAY	ZB M5
09:45	1176.00	1458.50	10372.00	-3.47	4311.50	36.9700	34.5100	114.01
08:30	1179.25	1462.50	10389.00	9.45	4318.50	36.6800	33.9100	113.30
09:00	1178.00	1461.00	10393.00	6.07	4315.50	36.9100	34.5700	114.04
09:30	1177.00	1461.50	10382.00	1.32	4314.50	37.0700	34.5880	114.04
10:00	1177.50	1459.50	10385.00	8.01	4317.50	37.0500	34.4800	114.02
10:30	1175.50	1458.00	10369.00	-8.58	4318.50	37.0000	34.3700	113.27
11:00								
11:30								
12:00								
12:30								
13:00								
13:30								
14:00								
14:30								
15:00								
15:30								
10:45:46	ES M5	NQ M5	YM M5	TTICK	AX M5-DT	AAPL	EBAY	ZB M5
COPY->	1175.50	1458.00	10369.00	-8.58	4318.50	37.0000	34.3700	113.27
ETR->	1176.25	1459.00	10376.00	-0.37	4321.00	37.0800	34.4200	113.28

FIGURE 4.2   RoadMap™ is my current tape reader. Technology has come a long way.
Source: www.dtitrader.com

TRADING IS AN ART

Trading is an art and not a science. The trading process is as intricate and delicate as the finest ballet. In fact, just like a ballet, the markets have a unique rhythm. There is a tempo for an up market and another for a down market. And there are times when the market's rhythm is so complex that the astute trader knows that it is not time to dance. If you want to be a good trader, you have to learn to understand the market's beat, and step to it.

Learning which numbers to watch and how to interpret them takes time and patience. To know that a stock is trading at a certain price means nothing unless you know something about where the stock has been trading and where it is likely to go from this point. Likewise, to understand an index, you need to know its key numbers, its highs and lows, how it generally responds during specific times of the day and the year, and its trading history.

It would be easy to get paid on Wall Street if there were a simple set of rules to follow. Just learn the rules, obey them, and get rich. A scientist works by rules. A scientist takes a known substance, subjects it to a series of tests, and identifies it. Or, the scientist can follow an established procedure and produce a known result. There is a proven method that is followed to get the same results time and time again. Trading is not like that. There are no set rules that always work. The market is dynamic; it changes with world events. If there is a political upheaval, if there is scarcity of a needed commodity, if there is a major technological breakthrough, the markets respond. But, the exact response cannot be known. The truth is, it does not even take a major event to affect market direction. Sometimes markets seem to shift for no particular reason at all. That is why trading is so difficult.

An experienced trader has identified the gauges to watch and knows the amount of importance to give each of them. An experienced trader has learned this through careful observation and experience. The learning process will not be easy and it will very likely involve some initial financial loss. If you are new to trading, do not expect to be profitable from the beginning. While you are learning, be prepared to lose some money. Without experience, it is very easy to be misled by incorrectly interpreting the data. The more you know, however, the less likely it will be that you will fall for the market's tricks. It's just like dancing. Keep practicing the steps; watch the swings and dips, and pretty soon you will be swaying to the market's rhythm and hopefully making money.

GET THE BIG PICTURE

Sometimes you can't see the forest for the trees. We all have heard the expression but we may not have realized its importance to us as traders. It is easy to look at one stock price or one indicator and form an opinion. If IBM is soaring, that must mean that a rally is beginning. Or, if Microsoft is reporting bad numbers, we should sell our high techs. Right? Such an approach is easy, but not very reliable because the opinion is formed with limited data that are not placed or evaluated within the broader context of the market.

In order to read the tape accurately, you have to analyze the information in context. I am able to put data in context because I keep a big picture of the structure of the market in my mind at all times. Day after day, I look at the big picture and remind myself of it. Then, I take my analysis from the big picture down to the month, the week, the day, and finally to the minute that I am trading. My system of analysis looks like a pyramid standing on its head. As the focus gets narrower, my analysis is honed in to the present market and the immediate trade at hand. Trust me, if you do not have some structure or framework to work from, you will not be able to understand the numbers that you are seeing and you will not be able to know what they mean. The rhythm of the market will escape you and every little false move that is made will lure you into a losing position. To read the tape accurately, get a big picture view.

KEEP A TREND LINE OF YOUR TRADING VEHICLES

As you already know, I start each year by recording the opening prices for every index, stock, or other market that I intend to trade during the year. Then, as the year progresses, I add each monthly open and each weekly open and connect the dots to make a trend line. If the line is moving up, I know the bulls are strong; if it is moving down, I know that the bears are no longer in hibernation.

I trade many index futures. When I consider the price of an S&P Futures contract, I consider that price in relation to my trend line. If the market stays above the yearly open, I consider there to be a general bullish tone to the market. The farther above the yearly open, the more bullish I consider the tendency to be. For example, if February, March, and April all have higher monthly opens, I note it. Then, I know to scrutinize bearish positions carefully. Figures 4.3 through 4.6 illustrate an example of my monthly trend line, on a weekly basis, for early 2005 for the S&P Futures.

Week Of	S&P	NQ	DOW
01/03/05	1213.50	1628.00	10781.00
01/10/05	1187.00	1570.50	10613.00
01/17/05	1185.00	1564.50	10560.00
01/24/05	1170.00	1510.00	10407.00
01/31/05	1176.75	1513.00	10481.00
02/07/05	1202.75	1537.50	10711.00
02/14/05	1207.75	1536.50	10813.00
02/21/05	1203.00	1518.50	10761.00
02/28/05	1204.50	1513.50	10775.00
03/07/05	1230.00	1540.00	10995.00
03/14/05	1205.750	1516.50	10818.00
03/21/05	1191.50	1492.50	10635.00

FIGURE 4.3   Weekly opening prices for the major index futures.
Source: www.dtitrader.com

As the trend lines in the example graphically show, domestic futures indices struggled in early 2005. Prices fell and none of the indices were able to return to the yearly opening price until sometime in mid to late February. As each week in January began, I was well aware that we were trading below the watershed yearly open. I knew that until the yearly opening price could be passed, any rally was uncertain. Therefore, I took long posi-

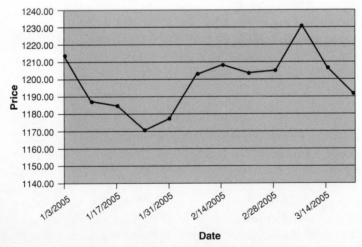

FIGURE 4.4   Trend line for S&P weekly opens.
Source: www.dtitrader.com

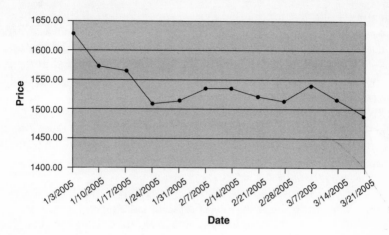

FIGURE 4.5 Trend line for Nasdaq weekly opens.
Source: www.dtitrader.com

tions with caution. Near the end of February, the yearly open was finally surpassed and I was certain that I did not want to be short because the strength of the bulls had been exhibited, at least momentarily.

Just because there is a bullish overtone to the market does not mean that I only trade to the long side. I let the numbers tell me what to do. Each day I look at key numbers (see Chapter 3 on key numbers) and I read the

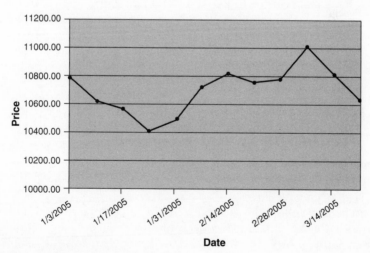

FIGURE 4.6 Trend line for Dow weekly opens.
Source: www.dtitrader.com

indicators. I put this information in the proper context. If the numbers tell me to go short, I listen. But if the big picture has a strong bullish overcast, I will not take a short position for the long term. I will short the market and take advantage of the down movement, but will be ready to shift my position when the indicators shift. Also, I will be more cautious going short if I know that the dance of the market is bullish.

By having an expansive view of Wall Street, I am less likely to be tricked by false moves. I am more cautious of moves that I know are contrary to the true disposition of the market. If I decide to take a trade that goes against the big picture bias, I look for confirmation of all my indicators. That way, I am better able to stay profitable.

Sometimes I miss moneymaking opportunities. That is true. But, I would rather err on the side of caution than frivolously throw my money away. If you miss a trade, do not worry. There will be another one. That is one redeeming thing about Chicago and New York: They always give you a second chance. Just be patient and wait for it. The market generally offers numerous opportunities each and every day.

Never Read a Price in Isolation

Stocks and indices rarely move very far from the pack. That is, if there is a market trend, all of the major markets tend to join it. If one or more of the markets is not coming to the party, be cautious because you may be misreading the indicators. For example, if the S&P Futures is trending up, expect the other futures indices to also trend up. If the Dow Futures is holding back and refusing to join the S&P in the bullish move, be careful. That could mean that the market's movement is momentary and not genuine. Wait for confirmation from the laggard before becoming a believer. If you take a position when you see market divergence, take a small one. Probe the market, but do not buy the farm. Divergence between indices and exchanges generally spells trouble.

For example, if the S&P Futures is moving up, the Dow Futures is moving up, and the Nasdaq Futures is also moving up, but the DAX Futures are refusing to move, it may be time for caution. Many times I have been saved because I correctly read the warning signal that was being sent by one lagging market. The old adage about birds of a feather flocking together goes for the markets, too. Generally, they trend together. That is one of the most basic keys to tape reading.

Stocks also follow the general trend of the overall market and their sector in particular. If pharmaceuticals are bullish, unless a corporation is experiencing a problem, its stock price will generally follow the established movement of the sector. There are, of course, exceptions. If a company is having a management problem, the price may lag. Or, if there is rumor on the street of an imminent merger, the stock may soar. However, in general, the rule applies. Most of the stocks in a sector will follow the trend of the sector.

Therefore, one of the first steps to reading the stock tape is to place the stock price in the context of its sector. If you are looking at Microsoft, how are all of the other high techs doing? If you are look at Merck, how are most of the pharmaceuticals doing? Never read a price in isolation. Always put it in the context of the sector and the overall market.

NOTE KEY NUMBERS

When trading a market, it is imperative that you know its key numbers. This fact is so important that one of the previous chapters is devoted to the concept. Knowing key numbers is essential to reading the tape. There is absolutely no way to properly read the tape without using them. You may want to refer back to the chapter on key numbers because they are that important.

Use key numbers for market entry, for protection, and for profit taking. For example, if you plan to buy an index, you do not want to buy it just before it hits major resistance. Likewise, you do not want to sell a down market just before a key support level. Wait and see how the market responds when the support number is hit because you must know if the down movement is strong enough to break through support. If support is broken, then it is time to sell. There is no sicker feeling than the one you get when you sell the daily low or buy the high.

The market usually follows the path of least resistance. Say, for example, that the market tries to move down and hits strong support. The market tries repeatedly to break the support but the bulls are too strong. Support just cannot be broken. Then you notice that a number of your indicators are shifting from negative to positive and the market looks as though it is gaining strength. Perhaps this is the time to buy. Support could not be broken; the bears tried but were not strong enough. I suggest you write this one down: A market that cannot move down will move up; and a market that cannot move up will move down. That is one of the laws of Wall Street.

If you are skilled at tape reading, it is possible to buy at the bottom and ride the market as it moves up. Some of my students have mastered this technique and it has paid them handsomely. Just be sure that you are reading the indicators carefully. This type of trade is very risky unless you are skilled. It is not a trade for an amateur. Be sure that you are dancing to the right tune and step lively.

CHECK MAJOR INDICATORS

A big part of correctly reading the tape is reading the market indicators. All experienced traders have indicators that they trust. Every day, I monitor several market indicators including two that I designed. Learning to interpret these indicators will enhance your trading. I list and explain the indicators I monitor and tell you how I read each indicator. The order in which the indicators are discussed is of no significance.

The Issues

The NYSE Issues is an indicator that reflects the number of issues that are above their previous day's close as compared to the number of issues that are below their previous day's close on the New York Stock Exchange. The Nasdaq Issues measures the same factors but is a Nasdaq indicator. I consider these indicators to be very important. When gauging the NYSE Issues, I believe 500 to be somewhat of a watershed number. If 500 of the issues are above their closing price, I will generally be looking more to the bullish side. Unless there is strong evidence to the contrary from other indicators, I will be hesitant to sell the market. Likewise, if the NYSE Issues is –500. I will be looking toward the short side. Again, unless the market has been far more negative and there is strong evidence that the market is reversing to the upside, I will be hesitant to buy the market with such a negative reading.

I always watch these two indicators. Sometimes the NYSE Issues will be strongly moving in one direction and the Nasdaq Issues will not follow, or vice versa. Such divergence raises flags of caution. Look for opportunities when both of these gauges are giving the same message. As I stated above, I consider the NYSE Issues and the Nasdaq Issues to be significant indicators and I always take them into account when trading during the daytime sessions.

The New York Tick (TICK)

Another indicator that I rely on is the New York Tick or the TICK. This indicator reflects the difference between the number of stocks ticking down and the number of stocks ticking up in price on the New York Stock Exchange. The TICK is a leading indicator for market direction. It is like the RPM gauge of Wall Street. If the TICK is positive, start looking up; if it is negative you probably want to consider the short side. A TICK reading of plus or minus 300 tends to be a neutral zone and is not affirmatively pointing in either direction. On the other hand, if you see a reading of plus or minus 1,000, the market has a definite view of things. The message is unmistakably clear. However, exercise caution because extremely high readings probably mean that the market is overbought or oversold. Generally, after the market reaches such levels, it needs to take a breather and there is a correction. The correction may be slight and it may be brief, but the market is unable to sustain a 1,000 TICK reading for a prolonged period of time. After a breather, if there is enough momentum, it may surge again.

I use the TICK as one indicator among a number of other indicators and criteria. I never rely upon any single indicator. Also, I read the TICK in relative terms. For example, if the TICK reading has been –450 and it moves into positive territory, say to a positive 200, the movement of the market is bullish. The number reflected by the reading is not particularly bullish, but in relative terms, there is some strength in the market. Perhaps a shift of some degree is in the making. Before taking any action, look at other indicators and check markets and indices for confirmation or denial.

The TRIN

The TRIN, which is also known as the Arms Index or Trading Index, measures volume and the previous day's close. The TRIN is a ratio of ratios. It is calculated as follows:

$$\frac{\text{Advancing Issues/Declining Issues}}{\text{Advancing Volume/Declining Volume}}$$

A TRIN of 1.00 is considered neutral. The lower the TRIN, the more bullish the indication; the higher the TRIN, the more bearish. Like the TICK, the TRIN is a short-term indicator. However, unlike the TICK, the TRIN is an inverse indicator. As the TICK moves up, the TRIN moves down and vice versa. The TRIN may go as high as 3.5 or as low as 0.30. Between 1.20 and 0.80 tends to be a noise zone in which no direction is indicated. When watching the TRIN, look at relative price action and not absolute value. For example, if the TRIN was 1.5 and it moves to 1.2, the direction is bullish even though the absolute value is slightly bearish.

Again, I read this indicator in relation to other indicators. Sometimes the markets will appear to be moving in a certain direction. For example, say that the S&P Futures moves up a point or two and some of the other futures markets join in the move. But the TICK and the TRIN are not showing signs of strength; they are telling a different story. I pull my hand away from the mouse and take a closer look. By reading the tape carefully, I am less likely to hastily join the potentially losing party.

MY INDICATORS

After trading for so many years, I designed two additional indicators. One of these is the V-factor; it records and reflects volume. The other is the TTICK. I designed the TTICK years ago. This indicator uses the TICK and the S&P Futures Index movement and merges them. It then smoothes out this information and numerically reports it. The TTICK and the V-factor are just two more indicators that I use and I think that they give my trading an edge over others.

The V-Factor

Volume is a very important characteristic of a really good market. With high volume comes liquidity. Most experienced traders use volume data in some manner when they trade. Generally, if a trend is strong it will intensify as volume increases. Likewise, as volume significantly wanes, it may be time to exit the market because the momentum is probably lost.

The V-factor records the volume and identifies the number of buyers and sellers. Then, the ratio is numerically expressed. The V-factor can be reset during critical times during the day to check the volume and the bias of the majority of traders during any trade zone or significant time.

Here is how the V-factor works: if the V-factor is 1.0, there are an equal number of buyers and sellers. If the V-factor is 0.5, there are twice as many sellers as buyers. If the V-factor is 2.0, there are twice as many buyers as sellers. I watch the V-factor while I am trading. If I am long in the market and the V-factor indicates that a lot of selling has stepped into the market, I may seriously consider exiting my position or lightening it. Use whatever program or method you like, but it is a good idea to watch volume when

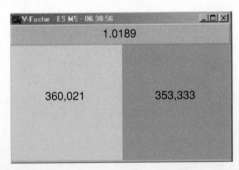

FIGURE 4.7   I use the V-factor, which I designed, to help me monitor volume.
Source: www.dtitrader.com

you are trading and take note if you observe large volume swings. A problem may be lurking in the background.

The TTICK

Some years back I created an indicator that I use every day. I call it the TTICK. It combines information from the TICK and the S&P Futures and synthesizes it and smoothes it out. The TTICK readings run from +30 to –30. A plus ten is an indication of a strong market. If the TTICK hits plus 20, the market is probably overbought and it may be time to exit a long position. Likewise, a negative ten is very bearish and a negative 20 may be a good point to exit a short position because the market may be oversold.

I use the TTICK and rely on it heavily for my trading. I correlate it to the other indicators and it guides my trading. For example, say that the TTICK hits +10 and I buy the market either in stock or in futures. The TTICK continues to rise and hits +15. The market is really moving up. Then, rather abruptly the indicators shift and the TTICK falls to +5. I may exit all of my positions. The TTICK is signaling to me that the market has shifted and there is no need to wait before I exit the trade. By watching the TTICK, I can better gauge entry points and exit points. The TTICK has made more money for me and my students than any other indicator. If the market data appears foggy, the TTICK is the ultimate judge for me.

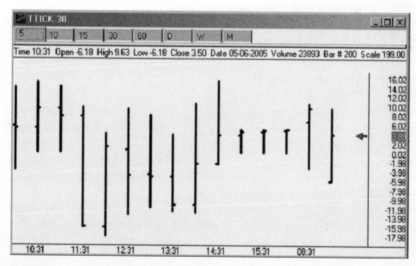

FIGURE 4.8   One of the indicators that I always watch is the TTICK. It is an indicator that I designed and I believe it greatly enhances my trading.
Source: www.dtitrader.com

You certainly do not have to use my indicators. Find indicators that are helpful to you and learn to use them. Market indicators are to traders like thermometers are to doctors. They let you know if there is a problem that needs to be addressed. If all is well, the indicators will tell you that also.

THE SIGNIFICANCE OF TIME

When I read the tape, I also consider the time of day. An entire chapter is devoted to the use of time in my trading method and I do not want to be redundant. However, I would be remiss if I did not tell you that when I read the tape, time matters. For example, if I see that a key number is broken and it is 1:45 P.M., I may not be too impressed. I know that this is the time of day that I refer to as the Grim Reaper time. The market is very volatile during this time. Bonds are going to close soon and the market often gives off false or short-lived signals. If it is not a trade zone for me, I very rarely place a trade. The market is just too hard to read during some times of the day and it is too easy to lose money. Therefore, remember that timing is everything and keep time in mind when reading indicators. I believe that the trade zones identified in Chapter 2 generally offer the best trading opportunities during the day session. During these times, I find it generally easier to accurately read the tape and get on the right side of the market.

TRUST THE NUMBERS

Anyone who has traded for any length of time knows that the numbers tell the truth. Do not rely upon your preconceived ideas or your emotions. If the numbers and the tape tell you to go long and the time is right, just do it. Forget about what you think or want. What you want to happen is irrelevant. The market does not really care about what you think. Just look at what is actually happening. All too often traders begin their day with a view of what the market should do. Then they plan their day and place their trades based upon their predetermined views. Often the results of such trading are disastrous. Our challenge is to put aside our views and our biases and let the numbers speak. Believe it or not, my Achilles' heel is experience. Sometimes I see a pattern that I have seen before. I form a bias about the market and determine what I think will happen next. This is a recipe for disaster. Never impose your bias on the market. Read and trust the numbers.

REVIEW

Trading is an art that is perfected over time. It is not easy to trade success-fully. Some people may try to sell you a system that claims to be simple and reliable. The system may work in certain market conditions and during spe-cific times. However, don't expect it to work for long because the market is a dynamic institution that is always changing. Trading is complex. The only way to win at this game is to learn to read the tape and to read it consis-tently and correctly. Education is the only real answer. The market has a rhythm of its own and you have to learn the points of support and resis-tance, the key numbers, the best trading times, and the market's indicators so that you can get in step with that rhythm.

Remember that you cannot read a stock quote, an index price, or a market indicator in isolation. The tape must be read in the context of the overall market. At all times, you need to keep both a big or long-term pic-ture and a short-term or current picture of the market in your head. That is the only way that you can read the tape correctly because you must put the numbers and indicator readings into that context. Look for confirmation of your moves from multiple indicators and multiple markets. If there is diver-gence, keep your hand off of the mouse.

Also, trade during the right time and read the indicators during the right time. Timing is important; an indicator reading may have one meaning at 9:00 A.M. and that identical reading may have another meaning at 1:30 P.M. Be sure that you get time working for you.

When reading the tape, keep the big picture in mind. Be sure that you have a clear understanding of the structure of the market. Let your analysis move from the big picture down incrementally to the moment that you are trading. Like a rifleman aiming at a target, set your sites and focus.

Chappy was right, the tape is all that matters. Learn to read it correctly and you will make money.

 LESSONS LEARNED

- Reading the tape is an art and not a science.
- The market has a unique rhythm. Move with it.
- Never read an index price or stock price in isolation. Put the data in the context of the market.
- Trust the indicators, not your preconceived notions.
- Watch key numbers and time of day when reading the tape.

CHAPTER 5

There's No Crying in Trading

S uccessful trading requires many skills. A good trader must know key numbers and understand their significance; a trader must use time advantageously; a trader has to correctly read the tape and that necessitates interpreting the market's indicators accurately. But, all of this is still not enough to be a winner. If you want to win at the trading game, you have to get your emotions under control and keep them on an even keel. Believe it or not, emotions play as big a role in trading as does accurate analysis. Letting your emotions overpower your reason will sabotage your trading every time. Correctly analyzing the market is simply not enough. The significance of emotional balance cannot be overstated. Recognize this fact and formulate strategies to deal with the emotional battles that you will wage when you are trading.

When your money is on the line, you will react to both winning and losing in a manner that you cannot predict. You may think that you will not be emotionally affected by market moves, but I assure you that you will be stunned by the power your emotions have and the difficulty you have in keeping them in check. Greed, fear, and arrogance are three of the most destructive forces that you will ever face in trading

A lot of traders do not understand this aspect of the game. They totally discount it. Their emotions are their Achilles' heel and it handicaps them so badly that they can never become winners.

DON'T GET GREEDY

Some, in fact most, traders have unrealistic expectations. "This year, I plan to make at least $1,000.00 to $2,000.00 a day as a day trader." Several years ago, that is what Andy, one of my new students, set as his profit target. I tried to communicate to him that his goal was too lofty. I bluntly told him that he was unrealistic. He was a new trader. He needed to work on managing risks and honing his trading skills. He had a lot to learn and he needed to be patient and set reasonable goals. Unfortunately, he abandoned my advice and continued to maintain an unrealistic hope of overnight riches in the stock market. Time after time I saw Andy enter a successful trade. His analysis was right and the market offered to pay him accordingly. Andy, however, would not take the profits offered. He wanted more and he held onto his position to get it. The market did not care about Andy's wishes. It often moved against him forcing him to eventually take a loss when he had earned a reasonable profit but refused to take it. Due to his greed, he lost money on winning trades.

If there is one thing I know about trading, it's that it is just like every other aspect of life: Setting realistic and achievable goals is one secret to success. Being overly aggressive in the market puts your assets at great risk and threatens your ability to stay in the game long enough to learn how to play it. When you enter a trade, set a realistic profit target and take your profits. Remember that your goal in trading is to make money. Always try to get paid. This does not mean that you always settle for pennies. It means that through proper analysis, you know when to take profits and you do it. Remember that you want to be a trader for the long haul. One trade is not your career; you plan to make thousands of other trades. So, have realistic and achievable expectations and enjoy reasonable profits.

Another young man had a very small amount of money in his trading account. He only had a few thousand dollars. Yet, he seemed to have a gift for trading. Often, he saw the big market moves and entered the market at just the right time to maximize his profits. But, he had one huge downfall. He did not know when to quit. He did not have much money and the markets heightened his greed. I actually saw days when, with such a tiny account, he made over $2,000.00 in a morning. That represented an almost unheard of return on his investment. Such a huge return, however, was not enough for him. He wanted more. After experiencing fantastic success in the morning, he traded in the afternoon and took even greater risks. Far too often, by the end of the day, he owed the market money. He lost everything he earned in the morning and then some. He had great potential as a trader but he could not control his greed. His greed caused him to enter risky trades and deplete his account. He had to give up trading because greed consistently got the best of him.

Don't get greedy. That is one of Wall Street's elementary lessons. When students come into my classes, we talk about goals. I ask them about their profit targets and financial expectations. There is always at least one student who expects to open a margin account with $10,000.00 and earn a million within a year. These traders do not comprehend the skill involved in making money in the markets and they do not respect the risks. There is a familiar saying among traders—pigs get fed and hogs get slaughtered. Greed will destroy a trader every time. Greed was my big downfall in 1987. I was busy counting the money I was going to make on my options and I was not adequately respecting the risks that I was assuming. I paid the price for my greed.

Holding greed in check is difficult. When the market is going your way, it is all too easy to get greedy. There is a natural tendency to want to maximize every trading opportunity and take every penny that you can from the market. By nature, traders are risk takers. They realize that there is money to be made in the markets. They know that every day the markets move up and down. It does not take a mathematical genius to do the calculations and determine that traders on the right side of the market can make a lot of money. The average range of the S&P varies, but is generally between 11 and 16 points. A skilled trader who buys the bottom of a bullish market in the morning and rides the market for its full daily range can pick up a tremendous return on his investment. One e-mini S&P contract bought at 1200.00 and sold at 1210.00 yields $500.00. Multiply that by ten contracts ($5,000.00) and the lure of the market is undeniable.

New traders are often too busy adding up potential profits to sufficiently respect the other side of that equation. Being on the wrong side of the market in the above example would result in a loss of $5,000.00. Don't forget that in order to make money you have to be on the winning team. That is, of course, the hard part. Even seasoned traders must always respect the consequences of overly playing a losing hand.

I have a degree in law. Earning a juris doctorate takes three years of intense post-graduate study. The tuition is expensive and the hours spent reading, researching, and writing are many. Geof Smith, my business partner and one of the instructors at my trading school, has a master's degree in engineering. He, too, wrote a lot of big checks to educational institutions and spent many years studying and working before he earned that degree. Yet, novice traders think that they can earn millions in the markets overnight without paying the price for education and experience. It does not happen that way. In the financial marketplace, just like in the courtroom, in the operating room, or in the board room, education, training, and experience pay off. Inexperience and ignorance are costly.

In addition to expecting too much from the market, greed can also blind traders to the truth. Greedy traders want to see a setup for profits.

They want to believe that the next trade will be the one to pay them. These traders enter the market with total assurance that they are right and that the market is going in their direction, even when the indicators clearly say otherwise. The market may be unequivocally alerting them to exercise caution, but greed blurs their reason and they take chances that they should never take and lose money that they did not have. Had they kept greed in check, they could have properly analyzed the market and waited for the right time to place the trade. Do not let your emotions get in the way of your analysis. As traders, we often want to impose our bias on the market, but we cannot. Most of us are just bit players on a huge screen. The big institutions may be able to exert some control over the markets, but we cannot. We are basically just along for the ride. Wall Street could care less about what we want or think.

Just remember that being greedy will not pay you. It didn't work for Midas and it won't work for you.

FEAR IS A NEGATIVE FACTOR

Greed is not the only booby trap waiting to ensnare the new trader. Fear is its all too-common partner. Being careful is always wise, but being overly careful and letting fear overwhelm you is lethal: It will paralyze you. Trading requires taking calculated risks. A trader who is afraid to take risks cannot succeed. That trader will hesitate and miscalculate. If too fearful, the trader will freeze and not be able to trade at all. Even when the market signals a buy or a sell, the trader is unable to click the mouse.

Here is how it works. A fearful trader buys ten e-mini S&P Futures contracts at 1202.00. The indicators support this move and the market starts to move up. The e-mini goes to 1202.50 and the trader is feeling great about the trade. The price rises to 1203 and the trader is sure that it is a big winner. Then the upward movement slows down. There is some resistance. Sellers step in and the market moves backward to 1201.25. What do the indicators say? They are all still giving a green or buying signal and supporting an upward move. What if the market goes to 1199.00? The trader will lose $150.00 on each contract. The trade still looks like a winner and the trader still has the indicators on his or her side, but he or she is afraid of loss. Maybe the indicators are wrong. Perhaps the trader miscalculated. Suddenly, fear takes over and without further analysis, he or she clicks the mouse and exits the trade. The trader accepted a loss of more than $350.00 on the ten contracts.

Seconds after liquidating this position, the upward momentum of the market returns and the market goes to 1205.00. The analysis was right, but fear took the money. Even though the indicators supported the position and the market had not proven the trader wrong, he or she threw in the towel because the trader could not manage emotions. Blinded by fear, the trader exchanged a nice profit for a loss. Fear won the battle.

Do not expect trades to always go your way. You will experience loss. No trader is right all of the time. Be prepared to accept and deal with it. Anyone who observes the markets knows that they do not move consistently in one direction over the short term. During the course of any trading day the markets move up a few points and back a few points. There may be stronger movement in one direction than in another, but there is always some consolidation and correcting. The winning trader has to learn not to panic every time there is a slight move against him. The trick is to correctly read the market and identify true shifts. Proper stop placement will help you do this.

Place protective stops slightly above or below resistance and support levels. Determine how much money you will lose on the trade if the stop is hit. If your protective stop takes you out of the market just be thankful, because if it was properly placed, you were wrong and you were on the losing team. You needed to exit.

Fear can also be so debilitating that it can keep you out of the market altogether. One day, after the market had dropped steadily like a huge boulder rolling down a steep and long incline, I noticed that during the entire trading day, one of my students had never sold anything. She had not executed even one trade. Even the inexperienced trader could have determined that the markets were falling out of bed and money could be made by selling just about anything. Yet, Jan had not placed a single trade.

I wondered how she missed the opportunity and I queried her about it. Jan sheepishly explained, "I thought the market was going down. The indicators were very negative and support was broken time and again. I saw that. I started to sell some e-minis, but I just was not sure that I was right. I was so nervous about making a mistake that I could not bring myself to click the mouse. I did not want to lose any money and I never placed a trade." Fear stole her profits while allowing the more confident traders the opportunity to take money to the bank.

The markets are driven by risks. Generally, the riskier the investment, the greater the profit-making potential that is offered. The key to successful trading is learning when the probabilities of success are on your side and taking advantage of that knowledge. You must take calculated risks. Don't be foolhardy, but do not be immobilized by fear either. Taking calculated risks is the name of the game.

ARROGANCE CAN ALSO BE COSTLY

Arrogance can also be a problem for some traders. They decide how the market is going to go. If the market has another idea, they don't even realize it because their arrogance blinds them to the truth. They have their head in the sand and cannot respond to what is really happening in the world around them.

I used to have that problem. I would buy some stock; say, for example, that I would buy IBM. If IBM prices fell, I just bought more IBM. If IBM continued to fall, I responded by buying even more of IBM. This method of trading is known as averaging down and, believe it or not, it is a method used by thousands of traders. In fact, it is a strategy that I used for years.

I remember the last day that I used it. I was trading the S&P Futures. At that time I always placed my orders in thirds. I bought the first third of my contracts. The market immediately moved against me and I was losing money. Fear reared its ugly head but I refused to acknowledge it. I responded by buying another third of my position. The market continued to fall and I continued to lose. It was getting harder and harder to stay calm and keep panic from sabotaging my strategy. My palms were wet with sweat, but I stuck to my plan and I arrogantly bought my final third. My losses kept getting greater and greater. I was getting sick.

On this particular day, the bears were clearly in charge and the market continued to fall relentlessly. My losses were increasing every second, but I just held on and waited for the reversal that I was sure was coming. I would not give in to fear and I would stick to my original plan, no matter what. After all, I was a professional and I knew how to analyze the market, right? I just needed to give the market time and it would validate me. Just hold the position and wait. This was no longer a trade, this was a war.

I waited for the market to shift and turn my way. I stared at the profit and loss box on the trading dome for what seemed like an eternity and I watched my losses increase as I sweated and my stomach flipped. My original arrogance gave way to fear and panic. I had not considered being wrong and I had no plan for dealing with the fear I was experiencing. I was immobilized. I felt like a pedestrian standing on a street corner watching an automobile headed straight for me, but I could not move to get out of the way. I was a sitting duck.

On that day, the market did not reverse and eventually my losses were so huge that the truth hit me and hit me hard. I could not deny it any longer. I was wrong! I had been a bull in a bear market and I could not buy my way out of my error. By adding to a losing position, I had only increased my losses and dug myself into a deeper hole. Those are the days you want to forget.

Losing is a part of trading. No trader is perfect. Even when you read the indicators carefully, even when you check and double check everything, even when other analysts agree with you, even when all of the news and statistics and reason support the position you have taken, sometimes you will still be wrong. Accept it and deal with it. As weird as it sounds, learning how to lose is really learning how to win because we will all be losers at one time or another. You must know how to deal with losses so that they do not defeat you. Winning traders put their bad days in perspective and keep on plugging away. They do not ignore their mistakes; they learn from them and get better and stronger.

One of my good friends, David, enjoys trading as much as I do. He is a great long-term thinker and has a good trading record. In January 2000, David started talking to me about a market correction that he believed was coming. He strongly believed that the market had topped out and that we were on the brink of a major market drop. His conviction was so strong that he put on a short position without any more thought. He had no real plan, no stop; just a powerful belief that he was right. At the time, David said that he knew he was correct in his analysis and he would hold his position regardless of the daily market moves. He was certain that history would prove him right. When it did, he would have a huge profit and be a hero.

I cautioned David about his actions. I told him that he should never be trading without a stop in such an all-or-nothing fashion. But, of course, he ignored me. Day after day, David's prediction proved false and the market moved up instead of down. David responded by digging his hole deeper. He started averaging up and continued to add to his short position even though all the indicators argued for a buy. David stuck to his plan for months; he was not going to be intimidated by the market. Day after day as prices went up, David's losses increased. Finally, on March 24, 2000, after several long and painful months, the Nasdaq broke all records and hit 4884; its highest price ever. Finally, David covered at the highest tick of the move and lost more than half a million dollars. David now uses stops; a lesson that cost him dearly.

I remember the anguish David suffered during those months and I remember how tormented he felt when he finally was forced to cover his shorts. He had to buy the market during a day when a record high was hit. It was a very torturous experience for him.

Do not be so arrogant that you cannot identify a mistake and deal with it quickly. If arrogance wins, you lose. David could have avoided a lot of pain, suffering, and monetary loss if only stops had been used, or humility had been tempered with arrogance.

Always Have an Exit Plan

In 1987, I did not have an exit plan. It was the single worst day of my life because I was at the mercy of the market. It took me over six years to get my emotional ship on an even keel. Eventually, I was able to analyze my past mistakes and take responsibility for them. I realized that my problems arose not because the market caused them, but because I caused them. I had no exit strategy. I did not respect risk in general and overnight risk in particular. Since that time, I have a tremendous respect for risk and when I enter a position I always have an exit plan.

TECHNIQUES TO TAME YOUR EMOTIONS

Over the years, I have learned techniques to deal with the emotional badgering of trading. I have developed ways to deal with both winning and losing trades. Greed, fear, and arrogance can all lead to destruction if you do not have an effective strategy to deal with them.

Set Realistic Profit Targets and Take Your Profits

All traders must establish realistic goals and take pride in reasonable profits that are commensurate with their experience and their risk tolerance. If money is left on the table, that is okay. There will be other trades and more opportunities to make money. Do not hold your positions until the market moves against you and your profits are gone. Get paid for your hard work.

You will not make a lot of money on every trade. Consider the following example. You put $10,000.00 in a margin account to trade futures indices. You make an average profit of $50.00 a day on your account. Some days you make more and some days you make less. There are also some days when you lose, but you manage risks and losses so that your average gain is $50.00 per day. In the course of a year, assuming that you trade 235 days, you have made over $12,000 before expenses. That means that you have doubled your investment. Few investment opportunities offer that kind of money-making potential.

Trading is a business. Treat it like a business. No one wants to work hard all day and go home empty handed. Do not let greed rob you of your profits. If the market goes higher after you liquidate your position, it is okay. Because at the end of the day you have made some money and you have profited from your skills.

Never Trade without a Protective Stop

Prepare for the worst and never trade without a protective stop. This is very, very important. Every trader makes mistakes. When you make a mistake, you want to be sure that you have limited your risk and protected your capital. Before entering a trade, determine the point at which you are sure you are wrong. How much will you lose if the market goes there? Are you willing to take that chance? If you are willing and able to take the risk associated with the trade, place your protective stop at the correct point. If the market hits your stop and takes you out, so be it. You were wrong and the market is telling you so. Trading without stops exposes you to unidentified and limitless risk. You just cannot afford to do that.

I was in the market on the morning of September 11, 2001. I was long and thankfully, I had my protective stop in place. The trade looked good and I was profitable. Pretty quickly the market shifted and took out my stop. I did not even know why. I asked someone to check on the news for me and see if there was something going on. Even though I had heard no news, the market was telling a story. Once the news spread, it was devastating for the market. My point in telling you this is that my protective stop saved me. I was not trading naked. I knew where support levels were established and I knew that if support was broken, I wanted out. Never trade without a protective stop!

Do not rely on mental stops. Mental stops are frequently ignored and an unnecessary loss is suffered. Trading is intense and it is too easy to be mesmerized by the market. Put a hard stop into the market and do not lose any more money on that trade than the predetermined amount. Never move your protective stop further away from the market. If market conditions shift, respond by moving the stop closer to the market. If there is a dramatic shift, exit the trade altogether. The goal here is to keep losses as small as possible.

The Two-Minute Rule

Another strategy that I often use to deal with a trade that is not working for me is the two-minute rule. Generally, if my trade is a good one, I know within two minutes because I am making money. A good trade usually pays me fast. Therefore, if I enter a trade and the indicators hesitate or change and I am not getting paid, I watch the clock. I have a clock built into my RoadMap™ software so that I can just click it and time my trade. If you don't use software, get an egg timer, an hourglass, or just a regular clock.

At the end of two minutes, if the trade does not look good and I do not feel positive about it, I get out of it. So what if the trade eventually works. Better to err on the side of caution than to give the market your money. Just exit and wait for a better opportunity. There will be other trades. Wait for them. Every day usually offers a number of good trade setups. There is no need to lose your money on trades that are not working. Think of it like this: Every single trade is just one of the next ten thousand trades you plan to make. Preserve your capital so that you will be in the game when the winners come along.

Plan Points of Entry, Exit, and Protection

Another technique that I use to keep my emotions at bay is planning. I form a strategy. Before I enter a trade, I have a profit target. When these targets are hit, I take that money to the bank. I also know where I will place my protective stop. How much will I lose if I am wrong? If I am wrong, the market will tell me by taking out my stop. I know that not every trade will be a winner, and I am primed for it. I am prepared for winning and I am prepared for losing. To be a winner you must learn from your losses and eliminate mistakes you have control over.

REVIEW

The mind is a very powerful thing. It controls both our emotions and our actions. Scientists are learning more and more every day about how it functions and the power that it has. Brain waves are so powerful that they can move a computer mouse. That is true. Scientists have designed equipment that allows a quadriplegic to communicate with a computer through concentrated and disciplined brain activity. That is so amazing. We all know that our brain controls how we feel and how we react to our feelings. But, to see the brain controlling something outside of the body is mind boggling! It is a real-life example of mind over matter.

Emotions and mind control play a big role in trading; a role that many traders do not recognize and deal with effectively. Do not expect your brain waves to move the markets up or down. I am not suggesting that mere concentration, no matter how intense, can transform a losing trade into a winning one. However, what I am suggesting is that the mind is very powerful and the emotions it generates play a vital role in the success or failure of your trading. Whether you believe it or not, it is a fact. Many traders psychologically sabotage their trading and they do not even know it. They are not prepared for the flood of emotions that sweep over them when they are trading and, therefore, they are unable to deal with them.

When the bank account balance is on the line, you will experience greed, fear, and denial. You will react in ways that you did not anticipate and, at least part of the time, you will take irrational and self-destructive action. In order to succeed as a trader you must prepare for the worst, just as a jet pilot must prepare for an engine failure. You must recognize the emotions that you will experience when you are in both winning trades and losing trades and you must be prepared to deal effectively with them. Design specific strategies for the market's movements and be ready to execute those strategies when your emotions get fired up. If you do not recognize the power of emotions in trading and if you do not prepare yourself to effectively deal with them, you will fail.

Do not destroy your next trade by worrying about and reliving your last one. If you plan to be a long-term player, there will be hundreds and maybe thousands of other trades. Work toward improving your skills and being ready for the next big opportunity. Enjoy the exhilaration of a good trade and avoid the misery of letting greed, fear, and arrogance take your trading account to the cleaners. The nice thing about trading is that you can always change and establish winning habits and become prosperous.

Over the years, I, like all traders, struggled with the fear/greed dilemma. Sometimes I have emerged victorious and other times fear or greed won the battle. If you recognize your emotions and acknowledge the power that they have over your trading, you have taken a big step forward. Then, design specific strategies for dealing with these destructive forces when your bank account is on the line. If you do that successfully, you will greatly increase the odds that you will be a winner.

 LESSONS LEARNED

- Educate yourself. Be prepared.
- Do not get greedy. Take reasonable profits.
- Tame fear. Do not let fear take your profits.
- You may be wrong. If so, admit it and exit the trade.
- Do not waste time and energy with regret. Do not demand perfection of yourself. Analyze your mistakes and learn from them. Then, move on.

CHAPTER 6

Riding the Rail

B eing lost is a miserable feeling. Traders without a proven strategy know how confusing and unsettling it is because they feel lost every day. They find themselves in trades that don't work, they wonder why they took the trades, and they respond by making more bad trades. They act impetuously, but don't seem to know how to stop. These losers approach the market like a ship of drunken sailors on liberty. They have no objectives and they get nowhere—except broke.

Always Have a Plan

Trading without a plan reminds me of an experience I had as a teenager in rural Tuscaloosa, Alabama. I had several older male cousins who lived in the area, and I looked up to them in awe. Their slightly advanced years allowed them to do exciting things that I could only dream about doing. They dated cute girls, drove fast cars, sneaked a cigarette or a little beer now and then, and generally did all the things I secretly longed to do. I was the baby; the one tagging along and taking the brunt of the jokes. Consequently, I was always striving to show them how big and tough I really was.

One summer's evening, I had my chance. I was visiting them and we decided to have a little fun. The night began innocently enough; we went to Leland Lanes, the local bowling alley, and played a few games. I worked hard to hold my own with the older boys and felt important just to be included. After a couple of hours at the alley, we decided to call it a night and head for home. However, as we walked outside, the rumbling sound of a nearby freight train caught our attention. We walked closer to the track to

73

get a better look at the long, slow-moving cars. The fascination of the rails was powerful. My cousins, Keith and Rod, suggested that we hop aboard and ride to the nearby trestle like they used to do when they were kids. I had never jumped aboard a train but it sounded exciting. I was both terrified and thrilled. My hands were sweating and my heart was racing. I reasoned with myself: It was just a train ride and the cars were moving pretty slowly. Surely I could jump aboard. No harm. This was going to be easy and it was going to be fun.

Suddenly, my cousins grabbed a ladder on the side of an old rickety car and faded out of sight. I hesitated briefly; I was shaking but the lure of the rail pulled me like a slab of metal to a giant magnet. If I did not jump aboard, I would be teased endlessly. Besides, I would miss all of the fun. I had to take this ride. Quickly, without any more thought, I grabbed the next car and hopped on. All I thought about was boarding the train. I never gave a thought to what would happen next.

Within seconds I realized the seriousness of my actions. I could not see my cousins and I had never been to the trestle where I was supposed to disembark. I did not know how far we were going to ride. I did not know how we were going to get home once we reached our destination. The bottom line was that I had no idea where I was going or what to do when I got there.

In addition to all of my other problems, I was not properly dressed. I was wearing wing tip shoes that kept slipping off the old iron ladder; forcing me to continuously readjust myself. Just as soon as I positioned my feet firmly and securely, we hit a bump or executed a turn and my shoes slipped again. As the train cut through the night air, I realized how chilly I was and wished I had a jacket. The cold went all the way to my bones. The night was pitch black and we were traveling through a thick pine forest. With the help of a little imagination, I saw wild animals and monsters behind every bush and tree.

The train was going faster by the second and I was getting more exhausted with every inch because I had to continuously work to stay aboard. I must have traveled at least twenty-five miles or more dangling off of the side of that rusty old car. My fingers gripped the rungs tightly as I pondered my options. I thought about jumping off, but the ground was whizzing past me. Besides, now I did not know where I was. I held on for dear life. I was certain that something horrible was going to happen at any moment.

For a long time, my fingers squeezed those rungs as I held tight and searched for that trestle. I listened for the voices of my cousins, hoping to hear them laughing in the next boxcar. But, of course, I didn't hear a human sound. As time passed, I began to wonder if they were dead; fallen from the train and crushed by the rails.

I was alone and there was no one to help me. I feared that I could not last long in my current position; especially with the increasing speed of the train. I decided to try to get into what I hoped would be a safer spot on the roof of the car. I carefully moved up the ladder one rung at a time. Slowly and deliberately I inched my way to the top. Once there, I searched for someway to hold onto the train. I stretched my arms outward in an attempt to get a grip on something and hang on. I lay flat and held on as best I could. The wind was whipping all around me and I was terrified. My body kept sliding from side to side and the train was shaking ferociously and bouncing continuously. If the situation were not bad enough, I suddenly saw a tunnel in front of me. I kissed the roof of that car; pressed my body down and prayed. I thought I was going to be squashed like a bug; painfully flattened on that old rusty rattling piece of steel. I held my breath and tightly closed my eyes.

I don't know how long I rode that train, but it seemed like hours before I caught a glimpse of some city lights. As I approached civilization, I looked for a landmark that I might recognize; something that could orient me to my surroundings. Finally, I saw a sign for the Jefferson Davis Hotel. I incorrectly assumed I was in Montgomery. When the train finally stopped, I was exhausted from the adrenaline racing through my veins and my knees were very weak. Somehow, I managed to use my wobbly legs and jumped off. Then, I just started walking; going nowhere, but moving away from the tracks. I was so disoriented I could hardly think, let alone speak.

I was quite a sight. My hair was coated in oil and grease and it was sticking straight up. My face was black and coated with dirt and soot. My clothes were stained with dirt and rust and I was trembling from the chilly night air. To add to my misery, I seriously feared that my cousins were dead; their bodies lying somewhere in those thick woods or mutilated on the tracks. I just kept walking away from the rail yard, dazed and trying to analyze the situation and come up with a plan. How could I get home without my father learning of my evening's activities? Dad did not put up with foolishness like this. I was in big trouble, really big trouble!

All along I thought I was in Montgomery, Alabama, but I was actually in another city 120 miles north of Montgomery. I was in Birmingham. I didn't get far from the track before a Birmingham police car pulled up beside me. The officers asked a lot of questions and I'm sure that they were quite amused. It was clear that I would soon face dad's wrath. Maybe my "deceased" cousins got the best deal after all.

I had to call Dad and tell him the story. The policemen made me; there was no option. I told Dad that Keith and Rod were probably dead, and he acted as though they were. He refused to come to get me or offer me any aid. I got not a word of sympathy. All he had to say to me was, "Get to the

Greyhound station and ride the bus. I'm not driving to Birmingham tonight. You got yourself into this mess, now get yourself out."

All the way back I thought about how I would explain to my aunts that their sons were dead; their mangled bodies lying somewhere in the piney woods between Tuscaloosa and Birmingham. I rued my audacious actions and promised God that I would turn over a new leaf.

That bus ride seemed to last for hours and my dread increased with each mile. When I finally walked into the house, I was fighting back the tears and my face was as long as that of an old hound dog. Much to my surprise, my cousins were waiting for me with plenty of jokes and comments. Even though they kidded me endlessly about catching the rail too slowly and being picked up by the police, I felt lucky to be alive and home. I was the dumb kid again, but it didn't seem so bad; not compared to the feelings of total helplessness and discomfort I experienced when I acted rashly without a plan. Being lost and powerless is not where you want to be.

Plan Strategically

Trading is a business and like any other business you need a plan. You can't afford to be lost in the woods. You would never launch a retail outlet or open a manufacturing facility without a plan and you should not begin trading without one either. First ask yourself a lot of financial questions and answer them honestly. How much money do you have to invest? Can you afford to lose it? How much money do you plan to make from your investment? Is that reasonable? Can you expect to make money right away? If not, when do you anticipate being profitable? Can you make more money elsewhere with your investment capital? What is your overall financial situation? Can you survive if you encounter problems with your trading? These are all important questions so take your answers seriously.

Also consider your temperament. Do you have the emotional ability to deal with risk taking and the feelings of loss? A trader must be a risk taker. Trading is all about risk. Winning traders take calculated risks and put the odds in their favor. However, no trader is always right. You will make mistakes and you will have losing trades. You may even have a series of losing trades. How will you react to them? Can both your pocket book and your emotional balance survive?

How much time do you plan to devote to trading? Will you trade full time or part time? During what hours will you trade? How will you trade? Will you trade online and execute your own transactions or will you use a broker? What vehicles will you trade? Do you want to trade futures, stocks, currencies, options? What are the different requirements of each and what are the different risks and rewards?

Most professions require training. Are you prepared or do you need additional training? Where will you get that training and what will be the cost? And training is not your only expense; what will your transaction costs be? How much margin will you need in your account? What will the equipment and trading programs cost? What other costs may be involved?

These are some of the things that you need to consider. After determining the answers, write a plan that includes your total investment requirements, your profit targets, your loss allowances, your expenses, and your time. Don't be lost like a teenager riding the rails in the dark. Know where you are going and how you plan to get there.

Strategically Attack the Market

A lot of traders enjoy being cowboys. They like the excitement of the ride and they don't worry if they have not prepared themselves for the unpredictable nature of it. They don't worry, that is, until their capital is gone and they are out of the trading business. Trading is hard and if you want to be a player for the long term, you must have objectives for your trading. You need an objective for every single trade. You can't just jump on board and hope for the best.

When you watch the market, it is easy to act impulsively. A few indicators signal a direction and before you know it, you have clicked the mouse and you're holding on to the seat of your pants while the market lunges up and down. If you have traded for very long, you have had this experience. Every trader has entered the market at inopportune times. The best way to control your thrill-seeking spirit is to have a plan of attack and execute it. My strategy for day trading futures and equities is a three-step system that I refer to as the three Ts of trading: the tick, the trade, and the trend. I use this method to limit my risks and increase my profits.

The Three Ts of Trading

I trade multiple contracts and I liquidate my position in sections depending on how the trade plays out. I call this approach the three Ts of trading and here is how it works. If I am trading futures, I purchase a number of contracts. For the purpose of simplicity; assume I purchase twelve e-mini S&P Futures contracts. My goal is to liquidate the first section (which could be one third, two thirds, or one half depending on the trade and the market conditions) of my positions with a small profit of only three fourths of a point or perhaps a point of profit. I refer to this part of the transaction as the tick portion. I only make a few ticks of profit. That means that in this particular example, if I start by taking off one third of twelve contracts I make about $37.00 or so per contract or around $150.00. There are now eight contracts remaining. The next step is what I call the trade portion of the position. I set my profit target two or three points above my point of entry (if the market will let me). If you remember the chapter on key numbers, you know that certain numbers are significant in every market. I locate the next key number where resistance will be anticipated and I sell a second part of my position at that point. If the next area of expected resistance is three points above my entry point, I place a sell order at resistance or a tick in front of it. When that point is hit, I liquidate the second portion of my position, or in this case, another third, which is four more contracts, and pick up another $150.00 or so per contract for a total of $600.00 for the four contracts. Now I have sold eight of my original twelve positions and I have made a profit of $750.00.

Now I am holding four contracts. This is the final part of my strategy, or the trend section of the trade. I try to hold these final contracts while managing my stop in hopes that the trend will continue. The S&P generally moves 10 to 16 points in a day. With a lot of planning and a little bit of luck, I can ride that trend and make some real good money on those remaining four contracts.

I always use protective stops. *Never trade without a stop.* (This is probably the tenth time I have stated this; get my drift? It is that important.) It is true that a stop is not a guarantee that you will be able to exit the market when and where you want. In a fast moving market, your stop may be skipped and the market may dive below your preferred exit level and leave you squirming. However, a stop protects you in most market conditions and using stops is the most basic and easiest step that you can take to preserve your capital.

When I enter the market, I know what my risks are with the trade. If I am required to place a stop too far from my point of entry, I do not take the trade because the risk is too great. I wait for a better opportunity. If I take the trade, I put my stop slightly above or below the appropriate key number (depending of course on whether I am long or short). As the market moves in my direction, I adjust my stop accordingly. After the trade portion of my contracts has been executed, I move my stop to a break even or better position and let the market finance my trade. Once you get to the point where the market is financing your trade, you are home free and can sit back and enjoy your profits.

In order to use the three Ts of trading approach, timing is very important. You want to select a time when the market is moving so that you will be able to liquidate a portion of your position very quickly. Hopefully, if you succeed in selecting the right time, you will enter the market just before it moves up or down and you will be able to liquidate the tick part of your trade very quickly. If the timing is right and the market is ready to move, within minutes, you may also be out of the second part of your positions. Then you can sit back and enjoy what I like to call a free ride. Or, if there is a shift in the market or major support or resistance is encountered, just take your contracts to the market and your money to the bank.

Do all trades work as well as the one just outlined? No. Sometimes, the market will not give up anything. But, some of them do work well. Other trades may partially work and you may get some small profits. The trick is to limit your losses and maximize your profits. You do not have to be right all of the time to win the trading game. However, you must exercise good money management all of the time. If you are wrong, you must have a plan for limiting losses and preserving capital. Chapter 7 discusses various aspects of risk management.

The three Ts of trading works for me for a number of reasons. First, every trader faces the powerful emotions of fear and greed. When we make a trade, we fear loss. We have all experienced it and we know that it hurts. Likewise, we all know the power of greed. When we enter a trade, we hope for success and the monetary rewards it brings. We do not want to settle for a two-point profit when we might get ten, twelve, or sixteen points. Yet, we know that greed can all too often lead to our demise.

The three-step process, as outlined, pays homage to both greed and fear. Because I fear that the market can move against me at any moment, I exit the first part of my positions quickly. By doing so, I have reduced my risk and made a small profit to cover any potential risk associated with my remaining contracts. If the market exhibits strong indicators that I am on the wrong side of the trade, I may be able to act quickly and exit my remaining positions with no loss or even a small profit. I am appeasing my fear by sacrificing a few contracts to it.

I can also enjoy greed. If I have selected the right point of entry and I am able to exit the first and second pieces of my positions profitably; I am holding my final portion with little to no risk. I have made enough money already to pay for the trade and cover any potential loss. I can sit back and let the market ride. If I have selected the right trading direction, I can enjoy watching the market move in my direction for hours and let my greed run wild. At any time when the market seems to really shift, I always have the option of exiting my positions and taking my profits. As the market moves in my direction, I adjust my stop and lock in profits.

I am comfortable with this trading strategy and overall it works well for me. I pick my points of entry and exit carefully. That is the reason that I watch time of day and key numbers so keenly. I want to enter the market when I have a good chance of getting a free ride.

Use the Three Ts in Trading Stocks

It is clear that I enjoy trading futures. However, during my career, I have traded equities, options, currencies, commodities, bonds, and just about anything else that I could trade if and when I saw the right opportunity.

Often I trade stocks and I use the same three Ts method. For example, I purchase three thousand shares of eBay, Amazon, or some other stock. If I were going to take the trade down in thirds, I would employ the following strategy. Sell one thousand shares very quickly and take only a small profit, say somewhere between 30 to 50 cents. In this way, I have made some money to help cover my potential downside. If the market turns against me and I suffer a loss on my remaining positions, I have some profit to offset the loss. If the trade keeps working, I liquidate my second third after a little larger profit, possibly between 50 to 70 cents per share. I try to get enough profit from the second third to put me in the position of being able to cover any loss that I may incur from my final positions. Once my downside is covered, I can follow the trend of the market because the market has covered my risk. I will place an arbitrary 1.00 stop to protect myself and then adjust it as the trade goes in my favor (or not). When the trade does, in fact, go my way, I have a free ride and no money can be taken away from me. I love getting into a free ride position. There is no fear and I can enjoy my win and my money.

If you are a beginner, be careful with this approach. Do not trade large amounts of contracts until you are able to trade one or two contracts profitably. If you cannot trade small positions and make a little money or break even, you do not want to increase your contracts. If you do, you will only succeed in losing more money faster. It is like the concept of the businessperson who loses money on each widget sold. If more widgets are sold, the losses are not made up with increased volume.

Tactically Execute

Having a strategy is not enough to make you a winner. You must execute the strategy correctly. Sometimes traders have trouble following their own plans. They may get greedy or anxious and enter the market too early, or they may hesitate and wait too long. If you miss the optimum time for entering a trade, it is usually just best to sit back and wait for the next opportunity. The trade may have been successful if executed properly, but a slow entry can turn a winner into a loser.

Because I use the three Ts of trading, it is very important to execute my strategy at the right time. My trade zones are the times during the day when my strategy tends to work best. This is true because there is generally greatest volatility and liquidity during the zones. Once I enter a trade, I want to be able to take the tick portion (approximately one third of my total positions) of my trade out of the market quickly and my trade portion (approximately one third of my total positions) out within a few minutes. Then, I can sit back without any risk to my capital and follow the trend of the market with the final third or so of my positions. If I enter the market when there are few buyers and the market is not moving, I have to sit and wait. I risk my capital until traders step back into the market. Then, the market may go my way or it may move against me. A slow market can be far more unpredictable for my method.

In addition to picking the right time, you have to also be sure that you identify the applicable key numbers and use them to your advantage. Do not buy the market just below a key resistance number or sell it just above a key support number. Look carefully before you leap. Also, use key numbers to identify your profit targets. If you are long and you know that the market is approaching a strong resistance level, you probably want to lighten your positions and take profits. If the resistance is extremely strong, you may want to exit your positions entirely and wait for resistance to be broken before entering on the long side.

Not only must you enter the trade at the right time, but you must also exit it at the right time. Just because you want to make six points on the trade does not mean that you can meet that objective. The market may be unwilling to cooperate. You have to set and accept realistic goals and exit your positions when the goals are met. In years past, I thought I could dictate my wishes to the market. Several years back when the average daily range was 20 points in the S&P, if I wanted six points of profit on an S&P Futures contract, I just held on and waited for it. With the 20-point daily range, six points was possible. But, the market changed and the daily range shrunk to about 11 points. My goal of six points of profit was too high. Perhaps I could have easily made three or four points, but not six. More times than not the market reversed before I got paid. It did not take me long to realize that I had to change my strategy to adapt to the market.

Watch the market, read the tape, and accept what the market offers you. I am not suggesting that you sell yourself short and bail your trades too quickly, but be realistic about your profit expectations. Don't expect the moon on every trade. If you do, you will be very disappointed and very broke.

Having realistic goals is the key. I remember going to high school dances as a teenager. If I went with reasonable expectations, I usually had a good time. But if I went expecting all the girls to fall down at my feet and everything to be exciting and ideal, I was disappointed and I came home feeling low. You can make a lot of money trading, but you won't do it with one trade or in one day. Keep expectations in line.

Never forget to keep a close eye on your indicators. Even if key numbers are being broken and the time seems to be ideal, if the indicators are signaling caution you had better heed their warnings. Check the NYSE Issues and the Nasdaq Issues, what are they telling you. Look at the TICK and the TRIN. Are they giving the same message as other indicators? How are other markets doing? Does the Dow agree with the S&P? What about the DAX? If one or more of them is lagging and refusing to join the others, wait. That is a red flag alerting you to go slow and take a second look. I cannot tell you how many times I have been saved because I looked at the Dow or the DAX and noticed that it was not moving in agreement with the others. The lagging market was giving the true direction.

The markets are very forgiving. They offer many opportunities to make money every day. If you miss one chance, wait and be patient. It may be a few minutes, it may be a few hours, or it may be a day or so, but the market will give you another opportunity. Just be patient, keep your powder dry and wait.

Many times trading is a patience game. Often traders think that just because they have the programs going on the computer and have been watching the screen for two hours, they have to trade. They feel that they have wasted their time if they don't get into the market. Trust me when I tell you, often the best action you can take is to stay out of the market. If the right setup is not there, you do not want to be there either. You want to have all of your money safely out of the market and you want to be an observer. Always remember that not clicking that mouse may well be the wisest and best trading technique at your disposal.

A final tactical issue to remember is that you must always limit losses. One chapter deals with risk management and preserving your capital. However, I want to mention it here because it is so important. If you want to stay in the trading game for very long, you have to preserve your capital. There will be times when you are certain that you are correct. You feel strongly that the market is going down and you sell. But, the market does not go down. Despite all reason and logic, it goes up. If the numbers tell you that you are wrong, listen and react accordingly. Just liquidate your positions and take your loss. You may not like it, but you may have to do it. Do not act foolishly and hold a losing position too long. Your losses will simply get greater and greater and before you know it, your account will be decimated. So what if the market ultimately proves you right and goes down. You can always sell it at that time. If you keep your losses small, you will be able to easily recoup them. If you stubbornly hold a losing position until you are taken to the cleaners, it may take days, weeks, or even months to get your money back. Proper risk management is very important. Never forget to treat it as such when executing your strategy.

The Markets Are Dynamic

Many beginning traders think that all they have to do is study the markets for a short time and find their secrets. That is, they think that they can identify something that will make money for them forever. They want some simple method or technique that is "fool" proof and will not change. Trust me. No such simple method exists because the markets are dynamic. They continuously change. A January market is usually quite different from a December market and a July market is different still. If there is an international crisis or a wonderfully beneficial event or discovery, the market may change. In times of high inflation or deep recession, things will change. The trick is to read the market and understand so that you can change with it. Learn the basic principles that undermine our financial universe and learn how to use this information in the marketplace. The proper education and training should help you stay on the right side of the market regardless of how it shifts.

REVIEW

Winners attack the market strategically. They have a proven plan of action and they execute their plan. My plan revolves around key numbers and advantageous times of day to trade. I also use major market indicators to determine the optimum time to trade. Then, I use a three-step approach. I purchase a block of futures or stock and I liquidate my positions in portions. I take the first section out of the market after only a few ticks. Next, I take out the second part after a point or two of profit. Finally, I maximize my profits with my final contracts and try to follow the daily trend of the market. I always try to get paid and I work hard to limit my losses.

I have a definite plan and I understand it and know that it works for me, but, having a plan is not all that counts. You have to execute the plan correctly. Know when you will trade. Know the signals that will alert you to be long or short. Before you enter the market, know where you will take profits and where you will place your protective stops. Calculate your potential risk. At what point do you know that you are wrong? How much will you lose if you are wrong? If you are unable or unwilling to take the risk, do not take the trade. If you take the trade, manage it. Keep your potential loss as low as possible and maximize your profits. Do not hold on to a losing position because you are stubborn or because the market casts its hypnotic spell on you. Let the indicators and the numbers tell you when it is time to throw in the towel or time to take your profits or losses and move to the sidelines. Once you have a strategy and you have tested it, execute it. Do not be hesitant or fearful. Just be sure that you are executing it tactically and correctly.

Some traders believe that all they need is a system. They will execute their system day in and day out, year in and year out. Let me assure you that that will not work. It will not work because the markets are dynamic. They are constantly changing. What you have to do is learn to read the markets and adapt to the changes. It takes education, patience, and persistence.

I have traded for many years. I have gone through fabulously lucrative times when my trading seemed golden. On the flip side of that I have gone through dark times when I felt like that foolish, impetuous and unsure teenager jumping aboard that slow moving freight train, lost in the midst of a dense dark forest. But, I have never given up. I know that the market is dynamic and ever changing. But I change with it. I read the tape, I follow the numbers, I have my strategy, and I execute it. Overall, my trading method works for me and keeps me winning the game.

 LESSONS LEARNED

- Have a proven strategy. Know how you will approach the market.
- Execute your strategy skillfully.
- Do not enter the market unless you know where you will take profits and where you will place protective stops. Always know your risk.
- Use a trading method that acknowledges both fear and greed, and manages both.
- Remember that the markets are dynamic. Adjust your strategy when necessary.

CHAPTER 7

Worry about Risk, the Rewards Will Come

The crash of 1987 taught me a major lesson about the art of trading: Manage your risk first and worry about your profits second. I know from experience that when I manage risk, the rewards come. Trading requires a long-term commitment. You have to be persistent, learn from your mistakes, and continuously improve. That is why risk management is so important. If you do not preserve your capital you will not have the staying power that you need to master the game and reap the real profits.

TRADING IS A BUSINESS

Day trading is a business. Just like any business, you have to manage it. Before you risk your first dollar, you must evaluate your personal financial situation. How much capital can you invest in this endeavor? Can you afford the potential loss? What is your age and what are the financial demands that face you. Consider these questions and others in the context of your big financial picture. Answer the questions honestly so that you are comfortable with the capital that you are investing in your trading business.

There are two reasons that you need to evaluate your risk tolerance. The first one is obvious; you must not risk money that you need for the mortgage or the car payment. We all know that such action is foolish. However, there is a second, equally important reason. As noted in the previous chapter, trading is a very emotionally charged profession. If you are risking money that you cannot afford to lose, you will not be able to concentrate on trading. You will be too fearful. Every time your account suffers a slight loss you will panic and be unable to rationally analyze the market and make a wise trading decision. Successful traders trade the numbers and let the market and not their fears guide their actions. Therefore, it is imperative that you be comfortable with the risks that you assume when you trade.

Next, you have to determine the cost of doing business. You will have to have the right equipment. Will you need to invest in a new computer? Do you want multiple computers and monitors? Personally, my system uses several monitors, but most of my students use only a single, laptop computer. At any rate, be certain that you have what you need or are prepared to purchase what you need. Also, you will need a data source. Trading requires up to the second, real time quotes that can be obtained for a monthly fee. Add this cost into your plan.

Then, there are your commissions. Commissions vary greatly from broker to broker. Some brokerage houses will overcharge and exact their pound of flesh. Shop around to get your best deal. Just remember that trading is not free. Don't overtrade and keep your commissions as low as possible.

Also, you need to be well educated and trained. Read, research, study, and continuously learn and improve. I highly recommend that you obtain some training before you start trading. I teach day trading classes and there are other educational opportunities available. Find some and take advantage of them. They are not free. You may think that the cost is too great. However, if you try to trade without an education, you will quickly learn that ignorance is the real expense of trading.

Recently a friend of mine relayed to me an experience he had while boating. He was in the Gulf of Mexico when his craft suffered some mechanical problems. He radioed for assistance and learned that the cost for towing him into port would be about $1,000.00. Jeff considered the cost and determined that it was just too great. He could have easily afforded the price but did not want to pay it. He believed that he could baby the engine, catch the currents just right, and make his way into port and keep his money in his pocket. Seventeen hours later, an exhausted Jeff finally drifted into the dock.

Jeff is a professional and time is money to him. Yet, he foolishly wasted hours of his valuable time because he was pinching pennies. I think that his cost benefit analysis was flawed. He would have saved a lot of money by paying the towing fee and arriving home in a timely fashion. He would also have been more comfortable and less stressed.

A lot of traders are like Jeff. They cut all the wrong corners. They turn pale when confronted with the price of a trading course because they assume that with their intellect, they will discover the secrets of the markets unaided. Why pay for instruction when their innate genius will keep them on track? (These folks need to read Chapter 11.) Intelligence—even genius—is not enough to beat Wall Street. At DTI, we always remind students that if they think the cost of an education is expensive, they should experience the cost of ignorance. Believe me, ignorance is expensive!

Educate yourself and learn all that you can about the trading vehicle of your choice. Only after you have a good understanding of how to trade, should you risk your first dollar. Even with a good education, trading will be hard.

Another problem is monetary loss. What will you do during the lean times when your trading does not make money? You will have periods of loss. I guarantee it. In fact, few traders are profitable immediately. I have never known a single person who began trading and immediately started making money. So, be prepared for the fact that you will not be reaping big rewards from your trading endeavors right away. In fact, it is highly likely that your initial efforts will cause you some degree of financial pain. Be prepared for it. Retail outlets open and close every day. If a retailer has only planned for months when sales are high and operating costs are low that retailer is in for a rocky road. The business will probably have a short lifespan. Be prepared for the slow times. Even experienced traders go through times when the trading is off. That just happens to everyone.

Remember that day trading is not easy. That is the reason you need to be prepared before you begin. It is well known that a significant number of day traders are out of business within a short period of time. They start trading with visions of sugarplums dancing in their heads. They do not respect risk and they do not have a sound business plan. They see trading as a get-rich-quick scheme and, unfortunately, they soon learn that it is not. From the first day that you trade, respect the market. Be well aware of the dangers lurking both within you (greed, fear, arrogance) and the dangers that are inherently part of the market.

For me, risk management involves a couple of different levels of control. First, I manage my overall account balance. I do not want my account to fall below an established level. Second, I manage my losses on each trade. Remember that how well you succeed in managing risks will determine whether you are a long-term player or nothing more than a flash in the pan.

MANAGE YOUR ACCOUNT BALANCE

Each trader has to determine the amount of money that he or she is willing to risk. I may be comfortable with one level of risk and you may be comfortable with another. Every one of us has to be aware of his personal particular risk tolerance and personality and act accordingly. I teach my students to determine the amount of money that they can lose without losing sleep. This dollar amount represents their "tilt" number. My tilt number will be one number and yours will be another. It depends on your particular financial situation and emotional disposition. However, the big idea is to determine a specific amount of money that is the most that you will lose in a day or in a trade and honor that number. In other words, how much of your account can you lose without really being bothered? Say, you have a healthy account balance and you can lose $5,000.00 and not suffer. Then, perhaps $5,000.00 is your tilt number. Another individual may have less capital and a $500.00 loss may be very uncomfortable. Therefore, $500.00 may be that trader's tilt number.

The important thing is that each trader must evaluate his or her personal situation and determine the loss that can be afforded and that can be accepted emotionally. Then, if the titlt number is reached during the course of any trading day, the trader must stop. Apparently, the trading techniques are not working or they were executed incorrectly. At any rate, the trader needs to quit, analyze, and regroup. Far too often a trader makes one or two losing trades and just continues even though the particular method or analysis is not working. Before the trader knows it, far more money than intended is lost and he or she is devastated. Once the mind focuses on losses, analysis is not clear and trading really goes down the drain.

Everyday I run a traders' chat room with my business partner and DTI's Chief Instructor, Geof Smith. As I began trading one morning, I immediately lost 25 percent of my daily tilt number. I gave the microphone to Geof and he soon lost the full 100 percent of the tilt number. It was only 10:00 A.M. but we were out of the game for the day. We followed our rules and did not trade anymore during that 24-hour period.

However, the next day, we still had money in our account and we were ready to come back and make the most of another trading opportunity. In fact, the next week was great and our trading yielded a good profit. The lesson here is that you must preserve capital and keep your account balance healthy or you will be out of the game. Stay in so that you have a chance to win.

One of the biggest mistakes that beginners make is focusing on a recent loss instead of concentrating on the current market. They always want to get their money back. With that mentality, they suffer a loss and then quickly jump back into the soup. They do not analyze and evaluate correctly. They take one bad trade and add a second and a third one to it. The market will always give you another chance but it may be hours or even days or weeks away. Wait patiently for it and take advantage of it when the time is right. Don't take just any trade. Take good trades when the odds are in your favor.

Another approach to establishing a tilt number is to set a percentage of your account balance that can be lost on a daily basis. Again, this must be a personal decision based on your specific situation. Some traders set a very low percentage, say 2 percent of their overall account balance. Other traders set a much higher percentage. In no case should you ever lose more than 10 percent of your total account balance in one day. If your daily losses consistently exceed 10 percent or more of your trading account, your trading life is definitely measured in days or weeks and not years.

Therefore, set a tilt number, either a specific monetary amount or a percentage of your account balance. Etch the number in stone. When the number is hit, stop for the day. Do not make any exceptions. Trust me when I tell you that this rule is very difficult; many traders simply cannot do it. They establish a tilt number but the tilt number means nothing. Day after day they violate their own rule and in a few days they are out of business.

Keep close tabs on your account balance and stay in the game.

Three Strikes and You Are Out

Another method of controlling losses that is used by some of my students is the three strikes and you're out rule. Regardless of the amount of monetary loss suffered on a trade, if the trader is wrong three times in a row, the trader closes the trading platform. Perhaps the three losses were managed well and it kept the losses very low. Nevertheless, the three errors in judgment signal that something is amiss. Timing is off, analysis is flawed, the market is unpredictable, or something. It is time to stop.

The three strikes and your out rule can also be applied to weekly trading. After three losing days in a row, take a break for the rest of the week. Things are not working for you so go play golf or tend the garden. The market is misbehaving and you do not want to reward it with your money. Many of my students have used this strategy to help them manage risks during periods of time when trading was very difficult and it has been helpful to them.

Always Know the Risk

Before you enter a trade you should know the risk involved. Where will the market need to go to prove you wrong? If it goes there, what will be your monetary loss? Are you able and willing to accept that loss? If you are not, do not take the trade. There will be other trades that involve less risk so wait for them. If you decide to take the trade, determine the nearest points of support and resistance. Use these points to establish protective stop placement and profit targets. Never enter a trade without having a clear understanding of your point of entry, your profit targets, and your point of exit if you are wrong.

There is one absolutely critical rule in trading: Never trade without a protective stop! It is easy to get into a trade with the intention of exiting the position if it does not work. You tell yourself that you will go to the market if the stock price drops to 99.25 or the S&P hits 1099. However, mental stops are too difficult to execute. You will find yourself giving the market more and more of your money. The market mesmerizes and hypnotizes you to the point of paralysis. Before you know it, you have lost far more money than you ever intended. In addition, there are times when the market moves against you so quickly that you suffer a major loss in the blink of an eye. If you do not have a hard stop already in place, there is no time to get it into the market before your account has taken a licking. Therefore, when you enter the market, simultaneously place a protective stop to be certain that you preserve your capital.

MANAGE EVERY TRADE

If a trade is working and you are making money, there is no problem. Just decide when to take your profits and enjoy them. If you buy IBM at 102.00 and the market goes to 110.00, no special skill is needed to take the money to the bank. However, if you buy at 110.00 and the price falls to 108.00, what do you do? How long do you hold your losing position? When the bottom line on the trade is negative, that is when real skill is needed.

Traders are risk takers. In fact, it is impossible to trade without taking risk. However, the risks assumed must be reasonable and must be in line with the potential rewards of the trade. Too often traders refuse to exit their losing positions simply because their egos do not want to accept defeat. These traders sit before their computers as if paralyzed and let the market take more and more of their money. Their trading involves a lot of wishing, hoping, and praying. They convince themselves that their loss is temporary and they refuse to acknowledge the warning signals that tell them that they are wrong. Eventually, after they have lost far too much money, they finally admit their mistakes and they exit their positions. The problem is that now their account is a lot thinner than it should or could have been.

Once I enter a trade, I keep my eyes on the indicators. If there is a recognizable shift in the market, I respond. That does not mean that I exit a trade every time I am slightly down. It does mean, however, that when the numbers and the indicators tell me that I have made a mistake, I acknowledge the mistake and exit the market. If the market responds in an unpredictable or inexplicable manner, I may exit my position even if I have not lost money. Over the years, I have learned what to expect from the market and I do not like surprises.

If the Market Is Unpredictable, Get Out

There are times when it is impossible to determine what the market will do next. It is just very unpredictable and trading is no better than flipping a coin. When you see these days or times, just quit. Stop and turn the computer off. Go play golf, work in the garden, or read a good book.

In 2005, Standard and Poors cut General Motors' debt rating. When the news broke, the markets went crazy. I watched as the S&P Futures Index melted from 1179.00 to 1169.00. As the train left the station, I watched from the sidelines. Risk was uncontrollable because the market was going up and down like a yo-yo. The market had been totally unprepared for this event and it reacted accordingly. Luckily for me, my experience had taught me to stay out of the market and watch while other less knowledgeable players were chewed up.

If you cannot tell where the market is going stay out of it!

USE PROTECTIVE STOPS

As you are aware, I always use protective stops. In fact, at DTI we have a cardinal rule: *never trade without a protective stop*! If my protective stop is hit, I believe that the market is telling me that I am wrong. I was long on September 11th but I had a protective stop in place. When the first tower was hit, the market responded negatively and my protective stop gently took me out of the market. Luckily I only suffered a small loss. Thank goodness I had a protective stop. Without it, my loss may have been great.

Also, once a protective stop is placed, adjust it as the market moves in your favor. For example, if you entered the market at 1102.75 with an initial protective stop at 1099.00 and the market moves to 1105.00, adjust your protective stop accordingly. Do not leave your stop at its original position and assume such a huge risk. Trail the market. In that way you reduce your risk and lock in profits.

Determining the point of placement for a protective stop is often tricky. There are several methods that can be used to determine the right spot. There are arbitrary stops, volatility stops, key number stops, and combination stops. The arbitrary stop is the least desirable and the combination stop is probably the most reliable. However, regardless of the stop that you select, choose one and use it.

Arbitrary Stops

An arbitrary stop means just what it says. Look at the market and pick a spot for a stop. Perhaps you decide that you will not give the market more than four points. Put a stop at the four point loss position. If you move the stop, move it closer to the market but never move it farther away.

The arbitrary stop is the most basic of stops and it is often used by beginning traders. Although it is not my stop of choice, I definitely recommend using an arbitrary stop rather than no stop at all. It offers protection and prevents major loss.

Volatility Stops

The markets are constantly in a state of flux. They move in one direction and then another. Generally, the market moves up and down between support and resistance. If the bulls are strong enough, resistance is broken. If the bears are powerful, support fails. Therefore, knowing the extent of the swings that can be expected can help you to place your stops. Look at some 30-minute bar charts. How low has the market gone within the last 30-minutes or the last hour? How high has it gone? Place your protection just above or below the volatility points. If your stop is hit, the market has broken out of its recently established pattern and a rough ride may be ahead. It is best that you are out, even if you must suffer a small loss.

Key Number Stops

Sometimes I use a key number stop. My RoadMap™ software helps me to determine the right spot for placement. I identify the numbers of support and resistance that are relevant to the particular market that I am trading. Then, I place my stop slightly above or below these levels. For example, if I am long a big S&P Futures contract from 1169.50, I know that the support level is 1167.60. Therefore, I place my stop just below that number. The market respects key numbers and if you know and use them, they are powerful trading tools.

The Combination Stop

This method uses all three of the previously discussed stops and selects the one that offers the maximum protection for the least risk. For example, if you are long the S&P Futures from 1169.50 and the arbitrary stop is four points from entry, the arbitrary stop is 1165.50. The volatility stop is 1167.25 because the market has gone that low in recent trading. The key number stop is 1168.90. The1168.90 stop offers the least risk and would be selected in this multiple choice approach.

Let the Three Ts of Trading Limit Your Risk

Another way that I manage my risks with each trade is with my three Ts of trading approach that I explained in the last chapter. I trade multiple contracts with the goal of exiting a portion (generally approximately one-third) of my positions with a slight profit; a second portion (generally approximately another one-third) of my positions with a slightly greater profit; and the final portion with a large profit. By taking some quick profits, I have managed to take some money out of the market to cover the downside of my trade. I have greatly limited my risk by getting the market to finance my trade. By using this approach I am able to reduce the risk of the trade quickly by taking some fast profits.

Remember that this multiple contract approach only works if you are skilled at selecting correct points and times of entry. If you are a novice and are consistently losing money, I do not encourage you to increase your number of contracts. If you do so, you will just lose more money faster. But, if you have enough skill and experience, the multiple contract approach can be very helpful to you.

Identify the Times that your Trading Is Weakest

Another thing that you may do to preserve your capital is to identify the times that are generally the best trading times for you and also identify the times that are the worst. If you trade during the times that generally give you a lot of trouble, be sure that you lighten your positions and exercise extreme caution.

Historically, Mondays are not good days for me. After taking many poundings from the market on Mondays, I now enter each Monday with my antennae up. I limit my number of positions and capital preservation is always at the front of my mind. By doing this, I have turned Mondays into low risk days so that my capital will not be eaten up before the week really begins. That way, I can trade later in the week when the opportunities are better.

FOLLOW THE TWO-MINUTE RULE

When a trade works, it generally works quickly for me. If my trade is good, I usually know it right away because my first profit target is hit in seconds and my second profit target is not far behind. Generally within two minutes I know whether or not I have a winner. I have a two-minute timer on my software that I set when I enter a trade. If the timer sounds and I have not been able to get paid on my first profit target, I reevaluate my position. I take a hard look at the indicators. Am I still happy with the trade? If I still have faith in it and the indicators and the numbers seem to support my belief, I hang on and give it more time. However, if there are danger signs surfacing, I take the trade to the market. Maybe the trade will shift and pay me, but the risks may be too great. It is better to exit if things are not looking right. You can always reenter after the picture is clearer. By exiting a losing position quickly, you can save yourself a lot of grief and a lot of money.

Set Realistic Profit and Loss Targets

Don't expect more from the market than it is likely to deliver. That is one of the biggest mistakes of beginners. They all seem to expect to get rich quick. The markets have an average daily range. Know the range of the market that you are trading. If the average daily range is 12 points and the market has already moved ten points, don't expect another ten points of movement before the close. There will be exceptional days, but the market will generally not pay more than its average daily range. With the S&P Futures, the average daily range runs anywhere from 11 to 16 points a day. Accept reasonable profits and take pride in them. Over time, small profits add up to a nice annual income.

Set a daily goal for success. If you are a beginner and you make several points of profit, you have done well. Take your profits and pat yourself on the back. Don't expect to make thousands of dollars every day. If you establish goals that are too high, you are only setting yourself up for failure and disappointment. As your skills grow, your profits will grow. Be patient and focus on learning and gradually making more money as your skills improve.

Also, set reasonable loss limits. I never lose more than one-third of the average daily range on any trade. If the average daily range is 18, I do not want to lose more than six points, or one-third of that range on any single trade. In fact, I very rarely lose that much on a trade. I evaluate my risks and watch the market too closely. I do not let losers deplete my account.

There are a number of ways that you can determine a market's average daily range. I use my RoadMap software to check the average daily range for the markets that I am trading. There are also web sites that will help you determine this information. One of my favorite sites is barcharts.com. This site is packed with useful information, including the average daily ranges for a variety of trading vehicles.

Know the Risks of Trading Futures

As you know by now, I enjoy trading futures and I have made a lot of money in the futures markets. One of the aspects of futures has always held a special appeal for me and that is leverage. Futures are highly leveraged investments. For as little as a thousand dollars, in a margin account, it is possible to trade the S&P Futures and control many thousands of dollars worth of assets. The e-mini S&P is worth $50.00 per point. Therefore, if you make ten points in a day, on one contract, you have made $500.00 on a $1,000.00 investment. Needless to say, that is huge. However, the downside is that if you lose 10 points on that contract, you have lost $500.00 or 50 percent of your investment. Leverage has one other downside. If you buy a stock at $100.00 per share and the price falls to zero; you have lost $100.00 on each share. But, futures are different. You can only trade with a margin account and you can actually lose more than your account balance. Your loss potential is not limited as it is with equities. If your futures account balance falls below the margin requirements, you will be forced to deposit additional funds to cover your losses. Therefore, many analysts consider futures very risky and day trading futures even riskier.

I understand the risks but I do not agree that it is necessarily more dangerous than a traditional buy and hold investment approach. I disagree for the following reason. I believe that the buy and hold strategy of many traditional investors is far riskier than my approach. It is a strategy based on blind faith because if the market goes down like it did in the early 2000s, these investors just sit on their hands and suffer. They watch their account go down day after day and do nothing. I, on the other hand, am a day trader and I adjust my trading on a daily basis as the market dictates. I believe that holding certain investments for the long term may be detrimental to my financial health.

As I noted earlier, the exchanges seem to support my position. If you trade a futures contract during the day and exit your position on or before the market closes, you have a much lower margin requirement than if you carry your position overnight. Generally, carrying positions overnight requires a significantly larger account balance. For example, it is possible to trade one S&P Futures contract for as little as $1,000.00, but if the contract is carried overnight, the margin requirement is $4,500.00. The exchanges know the risk of staying in the market and account for that risk in their cost structure.

Therefore, I trade futures, but I always use protective stops and aggressively work to manage my risks. I also never hold futures positions overnight. If I trade the night market, I enter the market once the night (Globex) session has started. I do not carry a position from the day session into the night session.

Manage Risk with Equities

I trade equities just like I trade futures. That is, I use the three Ts of trading approach. When I am day trading stocks, I generally purchase 3,000 shares. Then, I take a few ticks of profit with a portion of my positions. I trade the second portion and take more profit. Finally, I hold the final segment and follow the market trend. Unlike futures, I may decide to hold a stock position overnight if I have protective stops in place and if I have strong indication that I am on the right side of the market. Also, remember that if I have already exited approximately two thirds of my position, I have money in the bank to cover my downside.

When trading equities, just like when trading futures, determine the maximum loss that you will incur on a trade. Never lose more than 10 percent of your purchase price. For example, if you buy IBM at $100.00, set a maximum loss at $90.00 or a loss of $10.00 a share. Do not just buy and hold. Day trading is often criticized for its risks. Yet, buying and holding a stock without reacting to market conditions is a far riskier position to take. It is hard to accept a 10 percent loss, but that is far better than a 50 percent or greater loss. Do not bury your head in the sand, watch the market and react accordingly. When high-tech stocks fell in the early 2000s, millions of Americans just sat helplessly and watched their savings vanish. A lot of retirees lost most or all of their savings by holding on to a losing position for too long. Do not let that happen to you. Use stops and limit your losses. If there is a change in the market and the time is right for buying, you can always take the money that you kept and reenter the market.

Preserve Your Hard-Earned Capital

If you are wise, you will not only make money trading but you will take appropriate steps to preserve some of the money that you make. The ninth student who attended my school was a doctor from New York. At the end of the class, he deposited $20,000.00 into a trading account. He was apparently a very good student because at the end of 90 days, the account had grown to a half-million dollars. (Please understand that his great success was exceptional. Please do not begin trading with the expectation that you will reap such great rewards so quickly.) In the back of my mind I wanted to take credit for his success. But, I knew he alone deserved the credit. However, I did earn credit for advising him to preserve a portion of his capital. I insisted that he buy a certificate of deposit worth $100,000.00 and stash it away. My rationale was simple. With the money in the bank, he would never be a loser in the futures market. I did not want to see him succeed in taking a small amount of money, turning it into a small fortune, only to see him lose it. I wanted him to preserve some of his earnings for a rainy day. I hesitated to tell this story because I do not want all of you to think that in 90 days you can turn $20,000.00 into $500,000.00. Hank was an exceptionally good trader who possessed the skills he needed to win. He was able to use his skills and knowledge effectively and strategically so that he could tactically approach the market. Hats off to Dr. Hank!

I was proud that I advised Dr. Hank to put some of his hard earned assets aside. I advise all of my students to do that. Don't just keep all of your profits in your account; take a percentage of them out on a regular basis. If you don't, you get separated from your money and you get reckless. If you are profitable during the week, I suggest that on Friday you take a portion of those profits out of the account and place them in a checking account or some form of savings or investment. Trading income is hard earned so enjoy it. Always get paid.

GREEN CIRCLE COUNTRY

At DTI, we developed a very simple accountability system that we refer to as Green Circle Country. Each of us keeps a trading calendar. Every day when our trading comes to an end, we mark our profits and our losses on the calendar. If we are profitable by any amount, even one dollar, we place a large green circle on the day. If we have lost money, we draw in a large red one. That may seem very elementary and evoke memories of stars from the second grade, but it helps my students. My students work to stay profitable and green because they do not want to have to look at a calendar coated in red circles. I always tell my students that if they are green, even if by just one dollar, they are doing well and they are ahead of the game.

If you like the idea of Green Circle Country, get a calendar and get started. It is a simple way to hold yourself accountable for your trading results.

REVIEW

The primary goal of every trader must be to control and limit risk. If the risk of a trade is properly handled, the rewards will follow. There are a number of ways to deal with risks. I use a method of trading in which I limit risk by taking some quick small profits and financing my trade. I liquidate the first part of my position with just a few ticks of profit. I trade the second portion of my position and liquidate it with a two- to three-point profit. Finally, I use the final portion of my position to follow the daily trend and maximize my profits.

In addition to using the three Ts of trading, I always know the risk of every trade. If I am not willing to accept the risk of a trade, I do not take the trade. Also, once I enter any trade, I carefully monitor it. I always use a protective stop, but I watch the market indicators carefully and if the indicators shift, I act accordingly. I may liquidate all or part of my position and I may raise my protective stop, if the market signals to me that I need to do so. I do not just sit like a bump on a log and let the market zap me and take my money.

Some days are just difficult to trade. Maybe the market is acting irrationally and it is unpredictable and unreadable. Or maybe you had an argument with your spouse or learned that your mother is ill. Maybe you just don't feel good and didn't get enough sleep. Regardless, your trading is off and you just don't seem to be able to get in the swing of things. Quit. Stop. Turn off the trading platform and do something else. Every day will not be a winning day so deal with it effectively and limit losses on those bad days.

Remember that trading is a business and your capital is your inventory. Preserve your capital and stay in the game so that you can make money.

 LESSONS LEARNED

- Consider the risk of a trade first. If you control the risk, the reward will follow.
- Know the risk of every trade. If you do not like the risk, do not take the trade.
- Determine your personal tilt number and do not exceed it.
- Manage every trade to limit risk and control losses.
- Make preservation of capital your primary goal.

CHAPTER 8

Respect the News

Having a proven strategy and executing that strategy with precision ensures success. Right? Wrong. There is still one wild card that has the power to quickly sabotage your plans and destroy your business. That element is the news and you must not underestimate its significance. If Federal Reserve Chairman Alan Greenspan makes some unexpected public statements about the economy, expect the market to respond. When terrorists succeed in one of their diabolical plots, hold on because there is going to be a rough ride ahead. When a regularly scheduled significant economic report is published, expect the market to take notice. Nothing ignites or extinguishes the financial markets like the news.

Every trader needs to be aware of two types of news; breaking news events and scheduled economic reports. A news event may not sound economic, but it may, nevertheless, profoundly affect the markets. Political, social, and military events have the ability to greatly impact the financial and economic landscape. If an influential world leader is overthrown, if war is declared, if there is a peaceful conclusion to a hostile or volatile world situation, or if any of hundreds of other events occur, the financial markets will likely respond quickly and firmly. The impact of such news may be minor and fleeting, or it may be major and long lasting. There is no way to know in advance. News is the big unknown factor lurking above the market. Therefore, you have to prepare for news.

Obviously, breaking news surprises traders. There is no way to know that a terrorist attack will occur on a certain date or that a world leader will be assassinated. There is simply some degree of surprise that is inherent in trading; and the news is one such surprise. However, a great deal of economic data are published on a regular basis and it is possible to know when these scheduled economic reports are being issued. It just requires a little research and planning.

Various governmental departments and educational and financial institutions regularly issue a vast array of economic reports; the trick is in predicting the market's response to these reports once they are issued. Therefore, don't do it. As every trader knows, it is impossible to predict the market's response to news. Sometimes news will appear to be good, yet the market will respond in a negative fashion. On other occasions, the news will seem bleak, but the market surges up because institutional investors and the public were prepared for even bleaker news. Therefore, trading the news is risky business and I do not advise that you do so. I do, however, recommend that you be aware of the variety of economic news reported and that you always know when scheduled news is breaking. Again, educating yourself is the key. Find an economic calendar and check it before your trading week begins. You can get the information from *Barrons*, *The Wall Street Journal*, DTI, or some other source.

BREAKING NEWS CAN RUIN YOUR DAY

When I consider market moving news events that have occurred during the last several years, the most significant, bar none, is September 11, 2001. It was Tuesday and I had a class of advanced trading students at my school in Alabama. I do not remember the exact time, but sometime after 7:00 A.M. CST, we entered the futures market. The markets looked strong and the indicators reflected their strength. We were long the e-mini S&P Futures from 1098.00. The trade was going our way and the S&P had risen to 1102.00. Our protective stop was sitting at 1100.00 and we were sure we had money in the bank from this one. I was standing at the front of the class teaching. Our head instructor, Geof Smith was sitting with the students and watching the market data. In the front of the classroom we have a very large screen that displays our RoadMap™ software and gives us real time market quotes.

At around 7:45 A.M. Geof noticed that the market was acting oddly and he called it to our attention. The S&P had shifted and it had started moving down rather quickly. We had already taken some profits from the market and we had adjusted our protective stop with the upward movement of the S&P. As the market began acting up, our protective stop was hit. We were surprised and wondered why the market had shifted so fast. In the absence of news, it was an unusual move for this time of day. I have two TV's in my classroom that are on at all times. Although we are watching, we are not listening. Breaking news is very important in trading, and just knowing we have a watchful eye on the world is usually enough; but not on this day. There were no scheduled economic reports being issued at this time, but I knew there was news somewhere. I had seen this type of move before and I knew it was generally associated with news. So I asked Geof to step out of the classroom and see if there had been some breaking news.

A few minutes later Geof returned and notified the class that a jet had hit New York's Twin Towers. By this time the news had made it to the TV's in the classroom, and we saw the smoke and the destruction. But we were still not thinking about terrorists. We were thinking that some sort of accident had happened. Equipment had failed or a pilot had made a terrible mistake. We were aware that there was a problem, but we, like most other Americans, did not comprehend the extent of the situation. A few minutes later, we saw the second plane hit the remaining tower. Then we knew the nation and the markets were in real trouble. Fairly rapidly the S&P Futures fell to 1079.00. After a little fluttering, the price rose to the 1087.00/1088.00 range. But, we knew that this price was temporary, there would be a far greater price decline.

The big S&P futures contract ends electronic trading on the Globex at 8:15 A.M. CST. Trading reopens fifteen minutes later in the open out cry pits at the CME in Chicago. However, prior to the pit's opening, the New York Stock Exchange and the Nasdaq announced that they would be closed for the day. The S&P Futures responded by opening at 8:30 A.M. CST, but for only ten minutes. The Chicago Mercantile Exchange wanted to allow traders to exit their positions and clear their books because no one knew what might be in store for us. During those ten minutes, there was a flurry of activity and then the S&P followed the lead of the Nasdaq and the NYSE and closed for business.

The markets were closed for a week. They did not open until the following Tuesday. The world was shocked and saddened by the attacks and everyone needed time to clear their heads, consider the situation, and prepare for the markets to open.

On Tuesday, September 18th, before the markets opened, Greenspan held a press conference. He announced that the Federal Reserve was lowering interest rates. I think his comments generated even more fear and added another level of uncertainty to some already jittery markets. When Wall Street finally opened, things headed south and continued going down for days. On September 19th, the S&P Futures hit a low of 1017.50. On September 20th, the low was 938.50 and it just kept falling. By October 10, 2002, the S&P Futures bottomed out at 767.25.

The effects of September 11th were dramatic and long lasting. Remember our trade that morning, we bought the S&P Futures at 1098.00 and the market hit 1102.00. During the course of that year, the S&P fell over three hundred points. Of course, it was not just the terrorists that hit the tower. It was fear of other attacks, fear of war, and a lot of national uncertainty.

I did not know that our nation would face a disaster on September 11th. I began my day as usual and I executed my strategy as usual. Lucky for me and my students, part of my strategy is to always use protective stops. We had a position in the market, but we suffered no significant loss because we were prepared. As the market moved down it hit our stop and removed us from the market. I am a strong believer in the fact that the market will tell you when to exit a trade and move to the sidelines. If your protective stock is hit and you suffer a small loss, it is okay. The market is gently telling you that you are wrong. You made a mistake in analysis or in execution and you need to regroup.

Another breaking news event that I recently traded successfully was the second-term election of President George W. Bush. I knew that the markets were going to respond to the outcome of that race. On election day, I traded and I made money. As the election totals were released that evening, the market responded positively and I made more money. I was long and my profits kept rolling in throughout the evening. I had a strong feeling about the election. Apparently many traders shared my view and we were successful. However, even though I believed that I was on the right side of the market, I used protective stops just in case the market did not agree with my analysis.

Another trade that I executed off news was on the Sunday afternoon after Saddam Hussein was captured. I knew that the markets would respond favorably to the news. I bought the market when it opened and made money through out the evening. It is true that the markets did not follow through with their bullish move for long. However, I made my money when the fire was hot. Again, just in case I was wrong, I used protective stops. I was not totally exposed to the market's uncertainties.

Recall that I was an officer in the Air Force. In high speed jets, there are ejection mechanisms that allow pilots who face severe circumstances to eject from their air craft and save their lives. I have never had that experience, but I can only assume that having to eject is a fearful event. But, doing so may be the only way to save the pilot's life. Using protective stops is the day trader's ejection process. If unexpected news breaks and a trader is in trouble and headed for a potentially perilous situation, his protective stop can save him. He does not have to crash and burn.

It took a long time for the markets to recover from the terrorist attack on September 11, 2001. In fact, it took years. However, in late 2004, Wall

Street optimism pushed the markets up sharply and they again returned (even if only briefly) to those 1100.00 and greater levels that we were experiencing at the time of the terrorist attacks.

A DAILY MARKET MOVER: SCHEDULED ECONOMIC REPORTS

In addition to unexpected news events, there are many scheduled economic reports released each month. Some reports are compiled and released by educational institutions, some by industry watchdogs, and some by governmental agencies. I have selected about a dozen of the reports that I consider generally to be the most important to Wall Street. The order in which the reports are discussed does not reflect their importance. Sometimes a report will have a major impact on the markets and other times, the markets do not seem to care about that particular report, at all. It depends on many factors in the overall economy. Nevertheless, it is wise to know about these reports and know when they are being released so that you can prepare accordingly.

The remainder of this chapter discusses some of the most important regularly scheduled news events that you need to monitor.

The Federal Reserve Reports and Announcements

The Federal Reserve, or the Fed, was created during the presidency of Woodrow Wilson in 1913. The purpose of the Fed is to control the United States' monetary policy and serves as the nation's bank. It is a powerful agency led by a seven member Board of Governors who are appointed by the president and confirmed by the Senate. In addition to the Board of Governors, the structure of the Fed consists of twelve regional Federal Reserve Banks, the Federal Open Market Committee (FOMC), member banks, and advisory committees. The FOMC holds eight formal meetings each year. Alan Greenspan chaired the Federal Reserve from 1987 through 2005. When Greenspan spoke, investors across the world paid attention.

The Fed has several powerful tools used to control inflation, regulate the monetary supply, and keep the economy on an even keel. First, the Fed controls the discount rate. That is, it controls the interest rate charged to commercial banks and depository banks when money is borrowed from the Fed. It also establishes the reserve requirements for banks. It determines the amount of monetary reserves that member banks must keep to cover deposits. Finally, through its open market operations, the Fed controls the buying and selling of government securities to control the level of reserves in the depository system. If you want to learn more about the Federal Reserve System, their website is *www.federalreserve.gov*. The site contains a great deal of information including news releases, statistical data, reports, and other items that may be of interest to you.

As I noted, the Fed and its Chairman Alan Greenspan have the ability to affect the markets. Years ago, my friend David and I were sitting in my office trading the night market. We were both long on the big S&P. Everything was going well for our trade and we were sitting on the sofa watching a little television. David is a big guy. He is about six feet six inches tall and his weight matches his height. I, on the other hand, am much shorter and tip the scales at a significantly lower weight. (And, a lot better looking, I might add.)

Suddenly, Alan Greenspan appeared on the screen. Without warning he was addressing the media and commenting about the bullish market that we were experiencing at that time. For reasons known only to him, he referred to the rising stock prices as nothing more than irrational exuberance. I heard the words and I lunged for the computer. David was in my way, but I tossed him aside like a rag doll. My money was on the line and I knew it was in danger. Quickly, I grabbed the mouse and took our long positions to the market. I knew the market was about to dive and it did. My forceful and fast lunge to the screen saved us thousands.

Over the years, Greenspan has held many news conferences and appeared before the Senate and the House often. For some reason, he always seems to spook the market. Be careful; if he is speaking or if he appears get your hands on the mouse if you are in an open position. No individual seems to have more power to move the markets than Alan Greenspan or the current Chairman of the Federal Reserve. Being the chairman of the Fed is just powerful.

Another news event that you need to monitor is the press releases of the Federal Open Market Committee (FOMC). When each of the eight yearly formal meetings end, there is a press release noting the action, if any, that has been taken. During late 2004 and early 2005, there was consistent movement by the Fed to raise interest rates in an effort to stem the threat of growing inflation. The announcements of FOMC are very carefully watched and the market quickly and firmly responds. Know when the Fed is releasing reports and do not be taken off guard.

If you are a novice, I strongly suggest that you stay out of the market when the Fed is reporting. The market can move very quickly and be extremely volatile during these times. If you are on the wrong side of the move you will pay a heavy price. However, I confess that I have traded during or just after many of the Fed reports. Remember that I have been trading for about 30 years and I know how to get into and out of the market very quickly. I am not always right in my moves, but I have made money trading this particular news. Generally, I let the news come out and then decide, based on the market indicators, whether to be long, short, or out. If you are on the right side of the move, it can be very lucrative and you can make some nice profits in a short period of time.

Again, let me stress that the Fed is a huge market mover and if you are not an experienced trader who knows what to expect and how to respond, do not trade this news. Let the market digest it and settle down before you click the trigger.

Gross Domestic Product (GDP)

Another report that can deliver a whopping blow to the market is the Gross Domestic Product (GDP). The GDP is compiled and reported by the Bureau of Economic Analysis of the United States Department of Commerce. The GDP is generally considered to be the broadest measure of the general health and well being of the domestic economy. The GDP measures the total output of goods and services produced by labor and materials located in the United States. The GDP provides a panoramic view of the nation's supply and demand.

The GDP is released quarterly at 7:30A.M. However, advanced numbers, preliminary numbers, final numbers, and revisions are also regularly published. I suggest that you check the web site of the Bureau of Economic Analysis at *www.bea.doc.gov* to see when the various reports are being issued.

The GDP is an important report that is carefully watched by the public. It is used to detect early signs of growth or stagnation. Generally, if the GDP numbers are good and the economy is growing, investors and traders will be encouraged to join the bulls. However, if there is unbridled growth, it may arouse a fear of some economic problems ahead. Regardless, the GDP is an important report and every serious trader needs to pay close attention to it. I suggest being on the sidelines when these numbers are released. Let them come out and be digested by the market movers before you risk your account balance.

Consumer Price Index (CPI)

The Consumer Price Index (CPI) is the most widely used indicator to measure inflation. Each month the Department of Labor takes a specific basket of goods and services and determines the prices for those items if purchased in urban metropolitan areas. The basket of goods always contains the same items and includes food, housing, apparel, medical care, transportation, education, recreation, among other goods and services.

One can take the price of the goods one month and compare the price to the previous month or the previous year. The CPI is considered to be the most reliable reflection of inflation in the consumer sector. It is used by governmental agencies as well as by labor and industry to guide economic decisions. The release of the CPI may have a significant impact on Wall Street. If the numbers reflect high inflation, investors may fear a slowing of the economy as businesses and consumers are forced to tighten their belts and stretch their dollars. If inflation appears to be too high or if the financial markets are nervous, the release of the CPI may put the bears in charge. Or, if inflation is minimal the bulls may flex their muscles.

The Department of Labor releases the CPI around the middle of each month. The release dates should be available on the web site for the U.S. Department of Labor, Bureau of Labor Statistics. However, the release dates are sometimes changed. Therefore, check with *Barrons* (*www. barrons.com*) or some other source to determine the exact date of the CPI each month. This is an important economic release. Don't be caught off guard.

The Producer Price Index (PPI)

Like the CPI, the Producer Price Index (PPI) tracks price changes over time for a specific set of goods and services. However, there are some significant differences between the two indices. The CPI gauges consumer prices and the PPI gauges producer prices. There are thousands of PPIs. Every industry within the United States economy has a PPI. All of these individual indices are weighed and reflected in one big PPI that is released by the Department of Labor monthly.

One of the major uses of the PPI is as an early warning economic indicator. The PPI foreshadows price changes before they appear in the retail sector. This information is used for many things but one of its major uses is by the Federal Reserve in determining fiscal and monetary policy.

Like the CPI, the PPI is released on various dates, but is usually released sometime in the middle of the month. Also like the CPI, depending on the particular circumstances, the PPI may have a significant impact on the market. Know when it is being released and be prepared.

Michigan Consumer Sentiment Index (MCSI) and the Consumer Confidence Index (CCI)

Each month the University of Michigan conducts a survey to determine how consumers feel about the economy. The survey is designed to determine how consumers feel about spending. Are they buying cars, houses, clothes, and other goods and services or are they holding tightly to their purse strings? Five thousand households are surveyed each month and the final survey results for the prior month are released on the first business day of each month. A preliminary report is released on the tenth of each month, except for weekends.

The MCSI is a lagging indicator, that is, it is responding to how the economy has already changed. Nevertheless, it can be very important because it can confirm an economic pattern. Are consumers continuing to spend month after month? Or, are there signs of a recession and a pull back in consumer spending? Manufacturers, retailers, banks, and governmental agencies are some of the entities that may make financial decisions based on this indicator. If consumers are slowing their spending, businesses may decide to freeze hiring or reduce personnel. They may lower inventories or slow production. The reverse may also be true. If the numbers are strong, businesses may choose to expand and grow. They may invest more in production and personnel in order to meet consumer expectations.

Another measure of consumer confidence is the Consumer Confidence Index (CCI). These data are collected and released by the Consumer Confidence Board. Like the Michigan report, it is just a survey. There are no data collected on actual spending. Consumers are surveyed about their plans to spend or not to spend.

I know some traders who believe these reports to be nothing more than a bunch of hogwash. I have seen times when consumer sentiment data were released and the market did not seem to care. However, the market seems to respond to a noticeable change in consumer sentiment. Certainly a sustained pattern of confidence or fear by consumers is significant. Regardless of personal opinions, many analysts, who watch these numbers carefully, believe them to be important and very accurate.

As a trader, you need to be aware of when these numbers are reported. Do not make the mistake of being in the market without a protective stop when the numbers are released. You do not want to be taken by surprise by what could be a significant market shift. Again, there are a number of sources where you can gain information about the release. *Barrons* is one source. You can also visit my website at *www.dtitrader.com* where I publish a weekly and daily review of news releases for my students.

Construction Spending

The Department of Commerce gathers data about both residential and commercial construction. These numbers may be very volatile. That is, they may change greatly from month-to-month based on weather or other factors that effect construction. The numbers are also often revised significantly.

These numbers are released on the first business day of the month. The data released are for two months prior. The report is released at 9:00 A.M.

Again, these numbers can move the market. If the economy is already showing signs of strength, good numbers can add to the rosy picture. If there is some weakness in the economy, bad numbers can be the proverbial straw that breaks the camel's back. At other times, it seems that the market could care less. Just know when the numbers are being aired and don't be caught off guard.

Housing Starts

Housing starts differ from construction spending in that only residential units are counted. Single-family homes and apartments are tracked through the issuance of building permits. These numbers are also reported by the Department of Commerce. They are released at 7:30 A.M. during the middle of each month. This is a leading indicator. That is, it can be used as an economic predictor.

This is a tricky report to gauge. Regional data are gathered and compiled into a single report. The data can change because weather or a crisis in one region may alter the actual number of houses that are constructed. I live on the Gulf Coast and hurricanes can be a real problem for us. Consider the hurricanes in Florida. In 2004, that state experienced tremendous weather problems. Many houses that were planned were not built as scheduled and many other houses were rebuilt after having been destroyed. Other geographical areas may struggle with mud slides or earthquakes. All of these weather related events affect housing starts. Therefore, housing start numbers can be extremely volatile and revised significantly based on actual conditions.

One would think that strong housing start numbers were good for the bears: However, that is not always the case because when housing starts are very strong, it may signal inflationary conditions. The housing starts are closely correlated to interest rates. Generally, during times of very low interest rates, housing starts will be strong because money for housing purchases is readily available at low rates. High rates may put a damper on buying and building.

Again, housing starts are important and Wall Street looks at these numbers. Sometimes they move the market and sometimes they do not. Just be prepared to react to the market's response, whatever it is.

Institute of Supply Management (ISM)

This is a leading indicator that is used by both the government and economists. The report is issued on the first business day of the month. It measures both manufacturing and non-manufacturing purchasing. If there is a lag in industrial purchasing, there will be a slump in the economy. Again, this indicator can serve as a predictor of what the economy has in store during the months ahead.

This report can signal a slow down or a revving up of the economy. It can be a major market mover. Be sure that you remember to look out for it and its effect on the market.

Employment Cost Index (ECI) and Economic Situation

On the last Thursday of April, July, November, and January, the Bureau of Labor Statistics releases the results of its survey of employer payrolls. The report is aired quarterly and is released at 7:30 A.M. Central. This survey tracks the costs of labor, wages, and benefits for employers. If wages are rising, it may be an omen of rising inflationary conditions.

Another jobs report, issued by the Bureau of Labor Statistics, is the Report of Economic Situation. This report gives the unemployment numbers and the change in the unemployment rate. It also tracks the creation of new jobs. This report is very timely and is geographically broad and covers almost every manufacturing sector as well as industrial sector in the United States economy. It is deemed by many traders to be a good snapshot view of the overall health of the economy.

It has been my experience that during times when the economy is good, the market does not care very much about jobs reports. Other indicators take precedence. However, during poor economic times, job reports are watched carefully and if the numbers are bad, this report can tank the market. Watch out for it.

THE BIG IDEA: KNOW WHEN IMPORTANT REPORTS ARE BEING ISSUED

The Department of Labor, the Federal Reserve, the University of Michigan, and numerous other entities issue reports regularly. Before you begin your trading day, know the reports that are scheduled. I teach my students to always be aware of the news events that lie ahead. There are services that you can purchase that will give you this information. For example, my students have access to a report that I publish that is used as a premarket planner. It lists the scheduled news events and the times of the releases. Financial newspapers and magazines also detail this information. *Barrons*, a financial newspaper that is published weekly does a good job of detailing the financial reports from the past week and the reports for the upcoming week. Sometimes *Barrons* also predicts how the market will respond when the anticipated news comes out.

It really does not matter how you learn of scheduled news events. It matters that you know that the news is breaking and that you prepare for it. My general policy is that it is best to be out of the market when scheduled economic reports are published. Because some of these reports are major movers of the markets, you do not want to be caught on the wrong side of an avalanche. Often, as the news is released there will be a quick and strong market move. You may think that the market is going to soar. However, within minutes or even seconds it can shift and head down twice as fast as it went up. Generally, after the news breaks, it takes about three or four minutes for the markets to churn and digest the information. Then, exchanges begin to settle down and it is possible to analyze the data and their impact and get into the market, hopefully on the winning side.

REVIEW

News is extremely important to traders because news moves the markets. There are two types of news, unexpected breaking news and scheduled news events. It is impossible to predict breaking news. However, you do not have to be totally at the mercy of breaking news. You can and should always trade with a protective stop so that if an event happens, your stop will take you out of the market without a major loss. Remember the cardinal rule: NEVER TRADE WITHOUT A STOP!

Scheduled economic reports also move the market. Announcements by the Fed, the Department of Labor, the Department of Commerce, or other agencies or organizations are regularly aired. As a trader, it is your job to know when the reports are coming out and be prepared for them. My advice, especially for beginners, is to exit all positions before news is aired. If you do not have any positions in the market stay out until the news is broadcast and investors have had time to respond to it. Do not ignore the news. News is too important. Respect it and preserve your capital!

LESSONS LEARNED

- Be prepared for breaking news events by using protective stops.

- Each day, before you begin trading, check for releases of scheduled economic reports. Some of these events can send the markets soaring up or down.

- Stay out of the market when scheduled news is breaking. Let the market settle down before risking your money.

- Don't try to predict the news or its effect. You can't!

- Don't be lured into a market that is responding to news. The market may lunge up rapidly, but if the move is news based, it may fall twice as quickly.

CHAPTER 9

Getting Down to Brass Tacks

I have been trading since the late 1970s. Over the years, I specialized in the futures markets, especially the S&P and the DAX Futures, but I have traded just about everything at one time or another. In addition to futures, I have traded stocks, bonds, mutual funds, gold, oil, other commodities, options, currencies, and almost anything else that is tradable. In this section, I share the basic steps I take when I trade these securities. After each section, I give you the checklists that I use to make my trading decisions. I believe that an understanding of the S&P Futures is extremely helpful in trading a variety of securities. I use it to help me trade stocks, mutual funds, bonds, and other things.

In law school I learned a simple approach to analyzing issues and determining whether to be for or against a given proposition. As soon as I read the final examination question, I began my analysis by drawing a large capital "T" on my worksheet. On the left side of the T I listed the reasons that I should favor a given proposition and on the right side, I listed the reasons that argued against it. Then, I weighed and analyzed the two positions and decided whether to be ultimately for or against the proposition in question. Many people use the T-square approach to decision making within the business setting; I suggest that you use it for trading.

When determining how I will trade, I form a T and on one side I list the reasons for going short and on the other side, I list the reasons for going long. I have done this for so many years that I do not always write the factors down, but I always mentally go through the process. If there are as many reasons for going long as there are for going short, I just sit on my hands and stay out of the market. Now let's go through some major markets and let me explain the method to my madness.

TRADING FUTURE INDEXES

Rarely a day goes by that I do not trade the S&P, DAX, Dow, or Nasdaq Index Futures. I believe that regardless of the security you trade, it is important to understand the futures markets because they are often accurate predictors of general market direction. Obviously, my first trading decision must be to select an index to trade. If the broader market appears to be particularly bearish and one of the markets seems to be weaker than the others, I trade that market; the chances are that it will be the first one to go down. Conversely, if the general market is very bullish, and the S&P or Dow seems more bullish than the other futures markets; I will favor them. Always try to choose the leader of the pack and join it.

Second, I generally trade specific indexes at certain times. As a rule, I generally do not trade the Dow until after 9:30 A.M. I have found that it takes the Dow a couple of hours to decide where it is going. I want to let it make up its mind before I enter the fray. There may be exceptions, but generally that is what I do. If I trade the S&P, I usually do so from 9:00 A.M. until 10:15 A.M., or after lunch at 1:00 P.M. or 2:30 P.M. Again, experience taught me that these are the best times during the day for me to trade in this market.

I enjoy trading the DAX during the early morning hours. It opens at 2:00 A.M. and I trade it around 3:30 A.M., 6:00 A.M., or when I am trading the S&P. Remember that trading is an art. There is no absolute law. But, this is my rule of thumb. After many hours of trading, I have identified specific times that I generally prefer certain markets.

Put the Current Market in Context

You cannot trade unless you put the market in context. Is the broad market bullish or bearish? I use the annual trend line (previously discussed) to answer this question. If we are currently trading above the yearly open, I put a + mark on the long side of my T. That is one factor favoring a long position. If we are currently trading below the yearly open, the + sign goes on the short side of the T. I also look at the monthly open. Are we above it? If so, a mark goes on the long side. If it is below the monthly open, the short side scores a point.

Next, I look closely at the current market. I begin gathering some numbers. I want to know the high and low of yesterday's trading. I look at the S&P Futures to get this information. I also want to know yesterday's 12:30 P.M. number. How did the S&P futures trade during the night session?

What was the high and what was the low during the Globex trading? There are two other numbers that I gather. I get the DAX 6:00 A.M. price and the S&P 3:30 A.M. price. Then, I record all of these numbers and study them. Is the S&P currently trading above yesterday's close? Score one for the bulls. What about yesterday's 12:30 P.M. trading? Are we below it? Put a mark in the bear's favor? I go through the numbers on my worksheet and weigh them. Are the bulls or the bears showing strength?

Gather Key Numbers

As trading progresses, I look at the day's numbers. Where did the S&P open? Are we staying above or below the open? I look at the 30-minute bar charts. Is a bullish or a bearish pattern depicted? In relation to the last 30-minute bar, are we above or below it? By how much? I consider all of these numbers and tally the bullish points and compare those to the bearish points. Is one side winning the battle? If so, I look to join that team. Where is my point of entry? I look at my key numbers to make that decision. Where is the market exerting support? Where is it drawing resistance? I use my 30-minute bar charts, historical key numbers, and important trading prices like the daily open and yesterday's close to help me identify the key numbers that I should note. If I am buying the market, I place my buy stop just above the next identified level of resistance. I know that if the market is strong enough to break through that resistance, there is a good chance that it will move to the next resistance level. Likewise, if I am selling the market, I place my sell stop just below support. After support is broken, I know that the odds are good that the market will move down to challenge the next support level.

What Time Is It

Time is another major consideration. I want to trade during trade zones or during times when the market is apt to pay me. I don't like the sit and wait game. Time is so important that I devote Chapter 2 to it exclusively. Ideally, I get into the market and I get out of it quickly with some profits. I may stay in for a while with part of my position, but I do not want to be a sitting duck for the big boys. That is why time is so important to me.

What Do the Indicators Say

In addition to the numbers and the time, I look at the indicators. I explained previously the ones that I like to use. If I am buying the market, I want all major indicators to be positive. I like for the NYSE Issues to be at a healthy plus 500 and the Nasdaq Issues to be in a similarly bullish mode. I also want the TICK to be in a positive position. Preferably, I want to see numbers higher than 300. I also look at the TTICK (my personal indicator). If the TTICK is a positive 10 or higher, I know that there is strength in the current market. I do not know how long the bulls will be charging forward, so I want to take advantage of the move and get in and out with some quick profits. I also look at volume indicators. I prefer the V-factor that I designed, but use the one of your choice. As volume increases note how the market responds. Is there strength in the move that I identified? As I consider the numbers, each of my key indicators, and the time of day, I am making checks on the appropriate side of my big T (Figure 9.1). If there is a TTICK reading of +11, it scores a + on the buy side of the equation. Likewise, a −13 on the TTICK gets a check on the sell side. I consider how things are stacking up.

Confirmation

Once I am able to identify a market position, I look for confirmation or denial. I do this by looking at other markets. If I am trading the S&P, I look at the DAX and the Dow. What are they doing? If I am planning on buying the market, I want the other futures indexes to be bullish also. I identify the points of support and resistance in these markets and watch them closely. I want the DAX and the Dow Futures to support the position that I am taking and also break through resistance. I definitely do not want to see them fall and break support. If that happens, I know my long position is in trouble and I respond accordingly.

Obviously, you do not have time to check every number and every indicator. Check the ones that are most important and consider what they are telling you. Then decide whether to be long, short, or out of the market. If you are not sure, stay out. The markets are dynamic and there will be plenty of opportunities to trade. Err on the side of caution and constantly work on risk management. Remember that if you control the risks, the rewards will come.

Is There News?

Finally, before I click my mouse, I check for scheduled news events. I never begin my morning without knowing which financial reports will be released. Regularly scheduled news events are very important. If a major report is scheduled for 9:00 A.M., I sit on the sidelines. I do not get into the market until the news is broadcast, is over, and the market has a few minutes to digest it. I follow that same procedure anytime that potentially market moving news is being released. Breaking news cannot be controlled but scheduled news can be. Generally, within five minutes or so after a scheduled report is released, the market reacts and then it quickly settles back down. At that time, it is easier for me to determine the mindset of Wall Street and to decide what to do.

Consideraton for Long position

Positive	Negative
S&P higher than open	Nasdaq lower than previous mini-pivot.
S&P higher than previous mini-pivot	S&P below overnight High
Dow higher than open	Time, near end of TradeZone 1
Dow higher than previous mini-pivot	Dow below Key number 10200
Reference bar 3 broken higher.	News: productivity and cost

FIGURE 9.1   I used a sample T-Square to help me analyze my trades.
Source: www.dtitrader.com

Clicking the Mouse

Once I determine that the time and price are right, I am ready to place my trade. I explained my trading style in Chapter 6, so I just remind you of it here. I use a simple, three-step approach that I named the Three T's of Trading. This approach helps me balance fear and greed and also allows me to maximize profits while minimizing risks. I trade in increments of three and take profits at various levels. I make only a few ticks on the first portion that I liquidate and refer to this part of the trade as the tick. Ideally, I try to liquidate a third with a small profit. On the S&P Futures, I try to get .75 points; on the Dow Futures, my goal is 3 points; on the DAX, 1.5 points; and on the Nasdaq, 1.5 points. Next, I trade the next one third or so of my positions. My goal during this portion of the trade is 1.5 to 2.0 points on the S&P Futures, 6 to 8 points on the Dow Futures, 3 to 5 points on the DAX Futures, and 5 points on the Nasdaq Futures. If the market shifts quickly or the indicators signal danger, it may be necessary to liquidate more than one third of the contracts during the tick or the trade portions of the transaction. Always watch the market indicators and read the tape in order to react appropriately.

I never risk more than one third of the average true range of the market or index that I am trading. Once I have successfully liquidated the first two third of my positions, I move my stop to a break even position and evaluate. I can use this final portion of my trade to follow the daily trend. I may want to hold the position all day, or I may identify the next point of heavy support or resistance and liquidate my holdings at that time. At any rate, I move my stop to a point where I will not lose on the trade. With some luck and some skill, I may be able to hold the position until the market closes and maximize profits.

So, that, in a nutshell, is my procedure for trading the index futures. It revolves around key numbers, time of day, and market indicators. I constantly review the numbers and consider the context of the current market. I am not always right and you will not be either. The big trick is to manage your risk. When you are wrong, you do not want to sink the ship. Focus on keeping losses low and wins high. It takes experience to do that so start slowly and work on reducing risks.

A copy of my morning worksheet is included in the chapter (Figure 9.2). I teach my students to complete this worksheet each day before they begin trading. By gathering this information and studying it, you should be better able to analyze the market.

Previous Day's High				
Previous Day's Low				
Globex Open				
Globex High				
Globex Low				
Globex Close				
Weekly Open				
Weekly High				
Weekly Low				
The 3:30 Open				
Observed #'s				
Reference Bars	Open	High	Low	Midpoint
15:30–16:00 #1 S&P				
ND				
DJ				
3:30–4:00 #2 S&P				
ND				
DJ				
8:30–9:00 #3 S&P				
ND				
DJ				
12:30–13:00 #4 S&P				
ND				
DJ				

FIGURE 9.2   Morning worksheet.
Source: www.dtitrader.com

CHECK LIST FOR TRADING THE INDEX FUTURES

1. Choose a market
2. Get the big picture
3. Gather key numbers
4. Check the time (you want liquidity and volatility)
5. Read your indicators
6. Get confirmation
7. Check for news
8. Click the mouse

TRADING MUTUAL FUNDS

Millions of Americans are invested in mutual funds. Most of these individuals leave the trading decisions to the professional money managers hired to oversee the funds. Sometimes this is good and at other times it is a disaster. Fund balances may fluctuate dramatically, depending upon market conditions. I trade mutual funds and, of course, I have a hands-on approach. Here is how I do it.

I use a dual strategy. I allocate 80 percent of my account to more traditional mutual funds and 20 percent to index funds that allow me to go both long and short. One example of such a fund is Rydex. Rydex funds are specifically designed to allow a day trading approach to account balances. A maximum of two trades can be made each day with the Rydex Fund. There are other similar funds.

My profit target with mutual funds is 10 percent to 20 percent and the risk I assume is no greater than 5 percent to 10 percent. Those are my ideal numbers.

Focus on Diversification

With mutual funds I focus on diversification. Because these are longer term vehicles, I do not put all of my eggs in one basket. Obviously, I look for the funds that I believe will pay me. At the end of each year, I reconcile my accounts and determine what has been good and what needs to be discarded. I close out the losers and keep the winners.

At the beginning of each year, I look at the sectors and identify the best performers for the past year. I note the top ten and eliminate the top two of this group. This leaves me with eight sectors to consider. Remember, I am allocating 80 percent of my funds to mutual funds. Therefore, I allocate 10 percent of my balance to each of the eight funds. With a $100,000.00 account, it means that I put $10,000.00 into each of the eight accounts. Then, I watch and wait.

At the end of the first quarter, I evaluate my position. I take the worst three performers and reallocate that money to the best five performers. This allocation reduces my risk and puts my assets in the strongest funds that I have. I do this again after the second quarter. But, then I eliminate the worst two of the funds and reallocate my money into the top three performing funds.

By the time the second quarter has passed, I have narrowed the search for the best performing funds. Since my goal is to make 10 percent, once I reach my goal, I must make a decision; do I stay in the fund and ride it a little longer or get out? If it looks strong enough, I pull out half of my money and lock in 10 percent on half of my position. If the market looks like it is weakening up, I liquidate my positions and go to the sidelines.

Remember the T that I discussed at the beginning of the chapter. As I evaluate each fund quarterly, I am noting only one factor. Is the fund making money or not and how much is it making in relation to the other funds? My goal is to eliminate the weak funds and hold on to the strong ones.

As the third quarter ends, I again evaluate the three remaining funds. As before, I eliminate and reallocate. Since I only have three funds left, I find the worst performer, and reallocate those funds to the top two performers. I hold these into the end of the year. Once the next year begins, I start the process all over again.

Index Funds

You will recall that I only invest 80 percent of my account balance in these mutual funds and I reserve 20 percent to invest in index funds. I invest in index funds in order to hedge my position and to profit from a rising or falling market. My approach to index funds is different from my approach to traditional mutual funds.

I begin each year by recording the opening price of the S&P 500 and Nasdaq 100 Futures. I calculate a 2.5 percent deviation up and down from the opens. If either of these levels is achieved, I trade the index funds either long or short, as indicated. I evaluate which index is moving strongest in the direction of the market and I allocate my money accordingly. For example, if the Nasdaq is leading the market lower, and it is 2.5 percent down from its yearly open, I allocate two-third to three-quarter of my money into the short Nasdaq fund. I put the remainder into the short S&P Fund. This allocation allows for a higher rate of return or an off-set of the losses in the other mutual funds as the market falls.

If the market goes against me, using the previous example, I exit the position when the market goes 2.5 percent above the yearly open. I do not reverse the position and re-enter the market. I wait until the beginning of the next quarter and begin the deviation process again.

If the market is going in my favor, I evaluate at the beginning of the second quarter. I record the open of the second quarter and again calculate a 2.5 percent deviation above and below the open. If the market moves 2.5 percent against me, I get out. If it continues to go in my favor, I wait until the beginning of the next quarter and repeat the process again.

So, that is my approach to trading mutual funds. I diversify and I continuously monitor my funds and evaluate them. I make adjustments quarterly as needed to stay in the highest performers and get out of the losers.

CHECK LIST FOR TRADING MUTUAL FUNDS

1. Identify the ten top performing mutual funds for the previous year.

2. Eliminate the top two performers.

3. Allocate 80 percent of your account balance to the remaining eight funds.

4. At the end of the first quarter, close out the worst three funds. Allocate that money to the top five of your remaining funds.

5. At the end of the second quarter, reallocate. Close the worst two funds and add those monies to the top three funds.

6. My profit goal is 10 percent on any given fund. If I have achieved that goal at the end of the second quarter, I either close out the fund profitably or exit half of my funds out to lock in the 10 percent profit.

7. At the end of the third quarter, I eliminate the worst performer of my remaining three funds and ride my remaining funds to year's end.

8. At the end of the year, I go to cash and evaluate. When the new year starts, I start the process again.

TRADING STOCKS

There are many ways to maximize a trading day while trading the S&P Index Futures. One way is to trade stocks with price action that closely correlates to the S&P. Of course, stocks are equities and the S&P Futures are commodities. Therefore, they require two different accounts and are traded at different exchanges. Both may be traded electronically, but require different margin requirements, as well as different rules and regulations. The commission structures are also generally quite different.

I trade stocks both for longer term investing and for short-term day trading. At the start of each year, I identify ten high-performing stocks.

There are thousands of stocks to trade. I look for those that will trade best with the S&P 500, the Dow 30 Industrial Average, and the Nasdaq 100.

Once I select my stocks, I study them. That does not mean that I focus on fundamental analyses of earnings, P/E ratios, or cash flow. What it means is that I observe the stock to determine how well its price action lines up with the price action on the S&P 500. Specifically, how does it match up with the S&P during certain times of the day and year? Some stocks mirror the S&P 500 very closely; whereas others follow the same trend but tend to have rallies or corrections during specific times of the day session. I want to know this information before I trade the stock. So, I watch and learn. Before you trade a stock, observe it for at least a week and do not put on a large position until you probe it and feel comfortable trading it.

Three of the ten stocks that I always trade include the QQQQ, the Diamond, and the Spyder. These are actually stocks that are much like a mutual index fund. The QQQQ is an index stock for the Nasdaq 100, the Diamond is the same, but consists of Dow stock, and the Spyder is S&P stock. By identifying the support and resistance levels of the indexes, you learn a great deal about the stocks. When the S&P breaks resistance, you can buy the Spyder and trade it simultaneously. Or, conversely, sell the Spyder if support is broken. I especially like to trade the QQQQ. For every ten points of trading in the Nasdaq, the QQQQ will generally move about 0.25 points in the same direction. For example, if the Nasdaq futures sell off from 1543.00 to 1513.00, that is a 30-point drop and the QQQQ will probably sell off approximately 0.75 (Figure 9.3). On 1000 shares, that is a profit of about $750.00.

Index stocks have two main advantages over common stock. First, there is no uptick rule. With common stock, such as IBM, if a trader were to short sell 100 shares at the market, IBM's stock price would have to tick higher in price before the trader could sell the stock short. With the QQQQ, if a trader shorts the stock at the market, the order is filled immediately, and the trader benefits from the whole move.

Another advantage of the index stocks is that they are not so news dependent. It is true that economic news affects the whole market, but individual stocks are more vulnerable. If there is an SEC investigation or poor earnings, an individual stock may drop 10 percent or more overnight. Index stocks do not have earnings reports and CEOs don't get fired. Therefore, they are not as susceptible to many factors that affect individual stock holdings.

I make stock picks on the basis of both the strength of the sector and the historical performance of the stock. Some of the stocks that have consistently been on my list include General Electric (GE), Flowers Industries (FLO), Apple (AAPL), EBay (EBAY), Exxon Mobil (XOM), Amazon (AMZN),

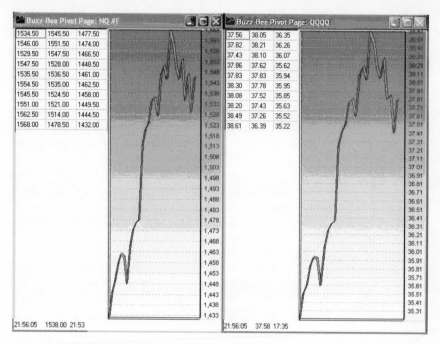

FIGURE 9.3   Note the correlation between the Nasdaq 100 and the QQQQ.
Source: www.dtitrader.com

Microsoft (MSFT), IBM (IBM), Intel (INTL), Wal-Mart (WMT), and Adobe (ADBE).

I generally stick with only large caps, except for companies listed on the Nasdaq. I want a stock that trades at least 4 million shares a day and has an average true range of $1.00. This is especially important for day trading because I need the ability to get into and out of the market quickly and I want the price of the stock to move within a reasonable time so that I can get paid.

Sometimes I buy the same stock for both longer term investing and day trading. In other words, in some cases, I will day trade a stock but I will also purchase shares of that same company and hang on to them for the long term.

Investing in Stocks

I begin by identifying ten high performing stocks. I note the yearly opening price of these stocks. I follow the stock price and record all of the weekly opens. I do not buy the stock until the price goes above the yearly open; I do not sell the stock until the price goes below the yearly open.

I study daily and weekly charts to identify levels of support and resistance. I do not want to execute a trade until the price of the stock crosses these points. In other words, if a stock is trading above its yearly open and I identify the next resistance point, I wait for resistance to be broken. Then, I buy and hold until the next resistance is reached. At least, that is the goal. Likewise, I may short a stock and I follow the same procedure, but of course I am looking for support to be broken and before I short a stock it must be trading below the yearly open. Once support is broken I sell and hope to stay short until the next support level is hit or until I reach my profit target.

I use the major futures indexes to determine market direction. That is, I look at the S&P, Dow, and Nasdaq to see whether they are heading up or down. For example, I recently relied upon the falling S&P Futures to short Research In Motion. I sold at $84.00 and rode it all the way down to $63.00 (Figure 9.4).

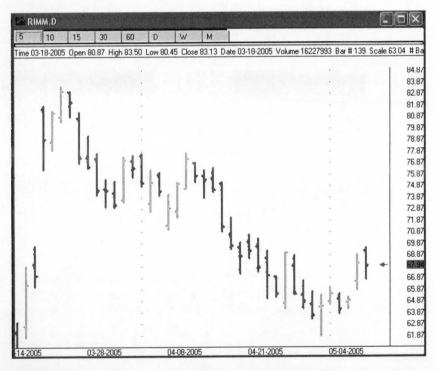

FIGURE 9.4   Note the movement of Research in Motion (RIMM) from $84.00 to $63.00.

Source: www.dtitrader.com

Day Trading Stocks

As you will recall from the previous section, I identify stocks that have a high correlation to the S&P 500 and those are the stocks I like to trade. IBM historically has a close price correlation as noted in Figure 9.5.

As you can see from the pivot charts in Figure 9.5, IBM mirrored the action of the S&P. Knowing this, though there was poor earnings news that sold off IBM ten points, a trader could have shorted IBM for a longer term while trading the S&P. Short selling IBM once it broke 100 could have yielded 20 points, in other words, 100 shares of IBM short from 100 would have yielded $2000.

While IBM mirrors the S&P, other stocks move in a contrary manner. For example, Coca Cola Co. (KO) tends to go down when the S&P goes up, and vice versa (Figure 9.6). Other stocks that move in a contrary direction include Anheuser Busch (BUD). By watching other stocks, you can locate others that correlate closely to the S&P 500 movements—either with the S&P or against it.

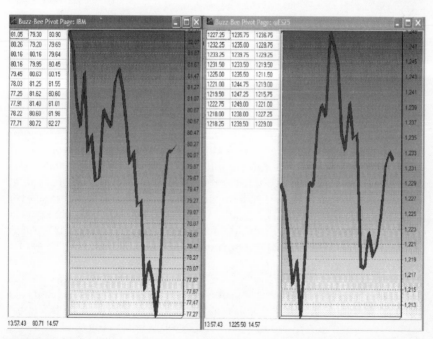

FIGURE 9.5 Note the close correlation of graph price movements of IBM and the S&P.

Source: www.dtitrader.com

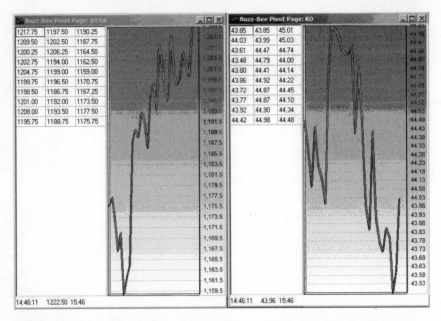

FIGURE 9.6 Note the inverse relationship between Coca Cola and the S&P.
Source: www.dtitrader.com

TIME AND QUANTITY

If I am day trading a stock, I always wait until after the first hour of trading because it is best to let things settle down. I always trade in increments of three, just like I do with the futures indexes. I usually transact 3000 shares. Once in the trade, I exit two-thirds or so of my position with a profit of 30 or 40 cents per share. Then, I pull my protective stop to either a break even position or the point where my maximum loss on all remaining shares is 20 cents. Then, I see how far I can ride. I always know the average true range (ATR) of each stock because the extent of the ATR is my profit target for the stock for the day.

Here is how it works. I purchase 3000 shares of EBay for $37.20 per share. I set my initial profit target for 30 cents on 2000 shares so I sell two-thirds of my position at $37.50 and make a gross profit of $600.00. Then, I have a 1000 shares remaining. I move my stop to allow for only a 20 cent loss. Even if I lose 20 cents on those shares, I am still profitable on the trade. Even with a loss on a portion of my positions, I have netted a profit of about $400.00 after my costs.

My goal, of course is to make a nice profit on the final 1000 shares by riding them up to at least the next level of resistance. With some brokers, there is a set fee for consummating a transaction, regardless of the number of shares traded. Therefore, you get more bang for your buck if you trade more shares. It is very economical for me to trade 3000 shares. You can use my method and trade fewer shares, but your costs will go up and your profits down.

Unlike the futures indices, there is not an additional charge for holding stocks overnight and sometimes I hold even my day trading stock overnight. However, if you short a stock, you can only hold it for three days before you have to begin paying interest. Also, if there is a dividend while you are shorting the stock, you have to pay the dividend.

Remember to control the risk before focusing on profits. When starting to trade stocks, do not start by putting on a full position. In other words, if you eventually want to start trading 1000 shares of Microsoft (MSFT) because you notice it has large moves in a day, start by trading 100 shares until you become familiar with it. This is the same principle as trading the S&P. Start by trading one E-mini and graduate from there. Once it is understood how it trades and its tendencies, increase your position or even start trading the big S&P. Control the risks and profits will come if you keep working to master your game.

Watch for News

Publicly traded stocks must report earnings and other vital information on a regular basis. Be sure that you keep up with the news regarding your stock picks and are not blind sided. Both good and bad news may have a major impact on price.

Protective Stops

Stops are critical in trading stock as with anything else in the financial markets. When trading stock, the initial stop placement must be above the high of the day if you are short, or below the low if you are long. As the day wears on, stops can be trailed using the RoadMap or the 30-minute bar chart. A trader will normally stay in a stock longer than in a futures contract and therefore, stop placement will generally be further back than it would when trading the futures. Key numbers can also be used for stop placement. Like the S&P, stocks have key numbers. By observing how a stock trades and by looking at 30-minute charts, a trader can determine support and resistance in an individual stock. Again, familiarize yourself with the stock before trading it.

CHECK LIST FOR TRADING STOCKS

1. Identify stocks with price movements that correlate closely to the S&P Index Futures.
2. As the year begins, identify ten of these that are high performing stocks.
3. Record the yearly opening price of each of these stocks.
4. Identify support and resistance levels for each stock.
5. If the major index futures confirm, buy when the price is above the yearly open and resistance has been broken.
6. If the major futures indexes confirm, sell when the price is below the yearly open and support has been broken.

CHECK LIST FOR DAY TRADING STOCKS

1. Follow the steps listed in the check list for trading stocks.
2. Do not trade until after the first hour of the session.
3. Watch for news and do not trade until any news settles.
4. Trade in increments of three.
5. Exit a large portion of your investment (two-thirds to three-quarters) with a 30 to 40 cent profit.
6. Initially place stop for protection as noted previously. After exiting two-thirds to three-quarters of positions, move stop to break even for the remaining shares.

TRADING BOND FUTURES

I begin preparation for my bond trading strategy when each year begins, but I do not execute a bond transaction until at least the month of April because I observe the price movement for at least three months into the year before I step into the market. I trade the 30-year treasury bonds. I record the yearly opening price. Then, I record a three-month moving average of all monthly opens.

Before I execute a trade I want two things to happen: I want the current bond price to be above or below the yearly open and I want the three-month moving average price to be in agreement with that direction. For example, if the bond price is above the yearly open and it is above the three-month moving average, I want to be a buyer. If the price is below the yearly opening price and below the three-month moving average, I want to be a seller.

Initially, if I am long, my protective stop is below the yearly open and the three-month moving average by about ten ticks. If I am short, my stop is above the yearly open and above the three-month moving average by about ten ticks. Bonds trade in 32-tick increments. Once I am profitable by about 5 percent, I move my stock to break even. Then, I keep a 5 percent trailing stop. That is, as the market moves in my direction, I follow it with my stop to lock in my profits.

As with all trading vehicles that are discussed in this chapter, before you begin trading them, study and observe. Bonds can be tricky. Learn how they move in relation to equities and the major indexes. Understand the inherent risks and do not focus solely or primarily on profits. Manage risk first.

The brief explanation encapsulates my method of trading bond futures.

CHECK LIST FOR TRADING BOND FUTURES

1. Record yearly opening price.
2. Create a moving average of each month's opening price.
3. Buy if the price is above the yearly open and above the three-month moving average.
4. Sell if the price is below the yearly open and below the three-month moving average.
5. If long, place protective stop below the yearly open and below the three-month moving average by about ten ticks.
6. If short, place protective stop above the yearly open and above the three-month moving average by about ten ticks.
7. Once profitable by 5 percent, move stop to break even.
8. Trail the market with your stop by 5 percent.

TRADING OIL OPTIONS

I trade oil with an option strategy only. Again, I note the yearly opening price and I do not trade oil until at least April. As with bonds, I record all monthly opens and obtain a three-month moving average. I look for the same criteria that I look for when trading bonds. I want to buy if the price is above the yearly open and above the three-month moving average. I want to sell if the reverse is true. If the market is going up, I do not buy calls; I sell puts. Likewise, if the market is going down, I sell calls; I do not buy puts.

My sole goal is to make money on premiums. If the strike-price of the options is not hit before the expiration date, the premium is mine to take to the bank. Therefore, I want to trade options that are no more than 45 to 60 days out from expiration.

I am trading naked options and there is a great risk involved. The risk, of course, is that the strike-price will be hit and I will be forced to deliver the underlying securities at the strike-price. Therefore, I want options that are about $5.00 or so out-of-the-money. For example, if the current price is $53.00, I will sell my puts at $48.00 and my calls at $58.00.

I do not trade oil all of the time. I look for optimum market conditions. Clearly, oil offered possibilities as prices soared in 2004 and 2005.

Remember that trading naked options is risky and I am not recommending that you do so unless you have some experience, understand the market, and have the funds to risk.

CHECK LIST FOR TRADING OIL

1. Record the yearly opening price.

2. Record monthly opens and create a moving average.

3. If the price is above the yearly open and above the 3-month moving average, sell puts.

4. If the price is below the yearly open and below the 3-month moving average, sell calls.

5. Only sell options that are 45 to 60 days from expiration.

TRADING GOLD FUTURES

I like to trade gold and I do so a fair amount of the time. I don't like to short gold, but that is not to say that I will not do it if the circumstances are optimum. However, far more often than not, I am a buyer and not a seller in the gold market. I prefer to hold gold longer than I do a lot of other commodities. That is, I like to hold it for anywhere from two weeks to six months.

Like everything else that I trade, I begin by recording the yearly opening price. Next, I record each monthly open and create a 65-day moving average chart. My strategy is very simple. If the price of gold is above the yearly open and above the 65-day moving average, I buy. If it is below the yearly open and below the 65-day moving average, I sell. Selling is not my favorite posture, but I listen to the market and the numbers and do as they tell me to do.

Once I am in the market, I place a protective stop below the average price for the last three monthly opens. My profit goal is $10.00 to $15.00 profit per contract. Once that profit target is achieved, I exit enough of my positions to cover any potential loss on my remaining positions or I exit the trade entirely.

I use several indicators to help me trade gold. First, I look at the dollar index. There is an inverse correlation between gold and the dollar. Also, I look at bonds. Again, I am looking for an inverse correlation.

CHECK LIST FOR TRADING GOLD FUTURES

1. Record the yearly opening price.
2. Create 65-day moving average.
3. Look for a profit of $10.00 to $15.00 per contract.
4. Obtain the opening prices for each month.
5. Place a protective stop below the average price of the last three monthly opens.
6. Once the profit target has been achieved, exit all positions or exit enough of your positions to move your stop to break even and ride the move for the remaining positions.

REVIEW

Because I consider myself an expert on trading the index futures, I use that knowledge to trade other vehicles as well. I believe that the S&P Index Futures can be used very effectively as an indicator for trading a variety of other securities. Over the years, I have used my knowledge of the S&P to help me trade stocks, mutual funds, bonds, and other vehicles. When I trade stocks, I select stocks that move in close correlation to the S&P. Some of the stocks that I trade move in the same direction as the S&P and mirror its action; whereas others move in a contrary direction. By reading the S&P, I am more enlightened about the market and better able to trade stocks. I employ a dual strategy of trading stocks for longer term investing as well as for short-term day trading.

With mutual funds, I focus on diversification and trade both broad-based funds and index funds. I select the funds to trade at the beginning of each year. Then, I equally allocate my account balance among eight strong performers. Each quarter, I revisit my selections and close out weak, non-performing funds and transfer those assets into the higher performing funds. Finally, by the end of the year, I have only a few funds, but they are my strongest performers.

With the end of the year, I go to cash and evaluate. I start the year by identifying ten high performers, eliminating the top two of those, and starting the process again.

I trade bond futures but I do not trade them until at least April. The reason for this delay is that I base my trading decisions on both the yearly opening price and a 3-month moving average. If the price is above the yearly open and that average, I am a buyer. If it is below those two criteria, I am a seller. I, of course, use protective stops and I always identify my profit targets before I enter the market.

I trade commodities, too. Two of my favorite commodities are oil and gold. I only trade oil using an options strategy. Like my bond futures method, with oil I also use the yearly opening price and a 3-month moving average to determine my point of entry. The goal of the strategy is to obtain premiums when the options that I have sold expire while they are out-of-the-money. Therefore, I only trade options that are 46 to 60 days from expiration. In a bullish bond market, I sell puts and if the market is bearish, I sell calls. Again, my objective is to obtain the premiums from selling the options. I sell naked options and this is risky. Be sure that you have a thorough understanding of all of the risks involved before you do it.

I use a slightly different approach to trading gold. I trade gold futures. I prefer taking the long position if the market allows. However, I will short the market if the numbers tell me to do so. As always, I begin with the yearly opening price and go from there. I record all opening prices for 65 days and obtain the moving average. Then, when gold moves above the yearly open and above that 65-day moving average, I am a buyer;. if it moves below those two benchmarks, I am a seller.

Remember to always do your homework and learn about any market that you trade. Always use stops and know your profit targets. Also, always consider risk first and profit taking second. If you consistently respect the risks of trading, you can learn how to be a winner.

 LESSONS LEARNED

- The S&P Futures Index is very important and can be used to help trade other securities.
- The yearly opening prices of stocks, bonds, and commodities are very important. Record the prices and use it throughout the year.
- Continuously monitor your mutual fund portfolio and adjust your holdings quarterly, as needed.
- Use a 65-day moving average to help you when trading gold futures.
- Do your homework and study a market before you trade in it. Know how it moves, identify its key numbers, and locate support and resistance.

CHAPTER 10

Preparation Pays

T he Boy Scouts have a motto, "Be prepared." I was not prepared for the events that took place on October 19, 1987. I missed all of the warning signals. Overvalued equities markets, an alarmingly high and rapidly increasing national debt, and high interest rates that Greenspan was raising to even higher levels. I should have noticed these and other warning signs, but I didn't. I simply did not see the huge red flags waving on the horizon. When the market crashed I was as vulnerable as a climber on Mt. Everest facing a blizzard without a coat. In fact, I didn't even have on a shirt.

My lack of preparation cost me dearly. I spent years regaining my financial stability and rebuilding my self-confidence. In fact, I had to start from scratch and regain my faith in the system itself. It has been a long hard road.

Since the crash, I have done a lot of soul searching and analysis. Today, when I enter the market I am ready—even for the worst. There is no substitute for preparation. Most of the time it is not the person with the highest IQ score who wins the trading game; it is the person who has prepared by accurately analyzing the market and being ready to respond correctly to it.

PREPARATION PAYS IN EVERY PROFESSION

A few years ago I met a lawyer in Mobile. John was a great guy but he seemed to have no more than an average intellect. Yet, he had a great record for winning cases. He won cases against some of the largest and most prestigious firms in town. I wondered how he did it. One day I asked another lawyer about John. "How is it that he does so well in the court room? He squares off against lawyers that appear to be far more intelligent and better resourced than he is. Yet, he wins almost every time. How can you explain it? I just don't understand."

"John's a scrapper. He makes up for any lack of intellect by working twice as hard as everyone else. He just outworks and out researches his opponents." That was the reply. John gained superiority because he was willing to pay the price to win.

All of us have seen people like John. They are totally dedicated to the task at hand. If you want to be a winning trader, that is what is required of you, too. You must be dedicated and you must prepare to win. It takes a lot of work.

Many people think that trading is easy. They will buy anything that purports to be the magic box. They do not understand the complexities of the market and the many skills that are required to succeed over the long term. They put a few thousand dollars in an account and believe that in a few months they will get rich. Sadly for them, it just does not work that way. The market chews them up and spits them out because to be a winner you must learn about all of the markets and take a global view.

The fact is that most new day traders will be broke and out of the game in a few months. Their account will be empty because they did not do their homework before they came face to face with the big boys. You do not want to be in that group. That is why you must be on top of your game. Only through preparation and hard work can you have a chance of beating the odds.

When you click your mouse and take control of futures contracts, stocks, commodities, or some other trading asset, you are entering into a highly competitive game in which some of the players are tremendously wealthy and very well trained. They may have millions of dollars at their disposal and the very latest technological tools to help them increase their chances of success. You, on the other hand, may have only a few thousand dollars to work with and may be sitting in a chair at your kitchen table using a dated laptop. That does not mean that you cannot win. However, it means that you need to work harder, learn everything that you can, and always be prepared. You are David facing Goliath and just as David had some powerful allies, so must you. Your allies must be your detailed preparation, accurate analysis, skillful execution, and above all, your money management. Everyday when you sit down to play the game, be certain that you are mentally and emotionally ready to win.

I admit that I sometimes get annoyed with some of my students who come to class unprepared. I remember one morning when class began at 5:00 A.M. We arrived early to learn a trade that I call the early bird. The students do a good deal of preparation for the trade and that includes taking a look at some of the foreign markets. We use this information to trade the S&P Futures. Like I said, class started at 5:00 A.M., at least most of us started at 5:00 A.M. One student was absent. We did the early bird and made a little money. Then, we shifted our attention to the German DAX. I like to trade the DAX Futures and there seemed to be a great set-up for a 6:00 A.M. trade. We discussed the market and did an extensive analysis. We were all sitting in front of our computers ready to click our mouse and buy the market when Gloria finally walked into the room. She missed all of the preparation and educational information about the trade. She had done no analysis and her equipment was not even set up. Nevertheless, she quickly got her laptop up and going and when we bought the market, she was not ready. It took her another minute or two to get everything together. Then, she clicked her mouse and entered the trade late.

The trade was very successful for all of us, except Gloria. She did not place her orders soon enough and got a bad fill with a lot of slippage. To make matters worse for her, our orders for profits were in the market before she got everything together. So, we got paid but the market shifted and dipped down before she could make a cent. Because she was not ready, she had a loser and the rest of us had a winner. We were ready to go when the trade presented itself and we got paid.

There are really two lessons to learn from Gloria's tardiness. First, get ready and be prepared. But, there is another valuable lesson as well. If you are late entering a trade for whatever reason, let that trade go by. You just cannot play catch up with the market. When you miss a great trade it is annoying, but chasing the market is never the right approach. Just let the trade go and get ready for the next chance. Keep your hand away from the mouse and be an observer.

DON'T GET COMPLACENT, KEEP LEARNING

In almost every occupation, it is necessary to continuously refresh your skills and stay on top of the latest research and developments. In Alabama, and in probably every state in the union, lawyers are required to take continuing legal education courses or they lose their license to practice law. Doctors have to know about new techniques, medicines, procedures, and even new diseases, or newly identified ones. I certainly would not want a doctor who had not kept up with the major advances in the medical profession to diagnose and treat me for a serious illness. Engineers also have to study and learn if they want to stay on top of the competition. Technology moves too fast for them to bury their heads in the sand and rely on the methods and knowledge of years gone by.

Trading is no different than any of these professions. Read financial publications, such as *Barrons, The Wall Street Journal,* or whatever you prefer, and know what is happening and when. Be informed about national and global economic trends. What are professional analysts saying about the market? You may not agree with them, but learning about their perspective broadens yours.

There are also a lot of books out there that can be helpful to you. Read some of them. Everything that you read will not be useful, but some of it will. If you gain just one or two helpful insights from a book, it is probably worth reading. Those insights might give you the edge that you need.

The internet is another great resource for traders. There are so many helpful web sites. Visit the Chicago Board of Trade (CBOT). You can locate it on the web at *www.cbot.com.* There is a lot of helpful information and resource material there. Also, go to the Chicago Mercantile Exchange (CME), or the NYSE sites. Look up stock reports or visit the Federal Reserve's site to get the latest reports and information. With all of the data and resources available today, there is absolutely *no excuse for not being an informed and educated trader.*

DON'T JUST READ BOOKS, READ THE MARKET

Remember that you do not trade unless you are familiar with the landscape. Without a clear understanding of the big picture, you are probably in serious trouble. Is the overall market bullish or bearish? You must know. As I explained earlier, I think that the best way to gain this insight is by forming a trend line like the one discussed in Chapter 2. Know the yearly opening price of the stock, bond, exchange, commodity, or other vehicle that you are trading. Keep records of each monthly opening price and each weekly opening price. Then, consider the daily price in relation to these numbers. Is the broad market moving up or down? How far above or below the yearly opening is the market currently trading? Let the numbers bring the picture into focus.

After you have a clear view of the market's direction, consider external factors. What are the economic stories that are dominating the news? Are they good or bad? How are they likely to affect Wall Street? Does the market appear to be responding appropriately to the general economic climate? In 2004 and early 2005, the really big story was the war in Iraq and the soaring oil prices that resulted from it. High oil prices strained budgets in many industries and clouded the national economic picture. Clearly, there was a direct correlation between these historically high fuel prices and the market's inability to seamlessly continue the rally that it experienced at the end of 2004.

So, step one in being prepared for market entry is conceptualization of the big picture. Obviously, if you are holding positions for any length of time, you want to be certain that you are on the side of the big picture trend. That is not to say that there will not be money making opportunities that go against the trend. Markets do not travel up or down in a straight line. Almost every day there will be dips or swings; if you are a skilled short-term player, you can take advantage of these opportunities. I do it all the time. Just be certain that you are making these trades within the context of the big picture. Otherwise, you will be tempted to hold your positions too long and overplay your hand. Suddenly, there will be a shift and your hard earned profits will evaporate before you can take them to the bank. Without a big picture framework you will also be vulnerable to every trick and false move designed by the big boys to lure you into the market on the losing team.

Trade in the Present

Once you see the big picture you are ready to take the next step and focus on the present. Where is the market today? What was the opening price? Do the bulls or the bears seem to be winning the day's battle? As the market trades, follow the key numbers to determine their strength. Can the bulls break through resistance? Can the bears erode support? I use a very simple 30-minute charting system described earlier. These easily readable charts help me answer the questions for the present. Once I gain an understanding of the short-term picture, I decide whether to be long, short, or out of the market and I act in accordance with my analysis.

It is hard to make the latter choice, that is, to stay out of the market. For some reason we always feel that we should be trading. We feel like we are failing or missing opportunities if we sit on the sidelines and watch. However, that premise is just simply not true. Sometimes the wisest thing that traders can do is sit on their hands and stay out of the market. If you are not going to make money on the trade, you definitely do not want to risk your capital needlessly.

In the past I over traded all the time. One of my biggest weaknesses is my love of trading. I just like playing the game. I like the excitement and exhilaration of being in the market. Trading is fun. It is one of the most exciting games that you can ever play. So, I continuously clicked my mouse.

In order to be successful, I had to really fight that tendency. In my early years I spent about 10 percent of my time thinking and 90 percent trading. As I became wiser, I shifted those percentages. Now I think about 90 percent of the time and trade about 10 percent. Always trade in the present; but only after being certain that the odds are in your favor. I am very selective with my entries because I do not simply want to play, I want to win.

A lot of traders cannot trade in the present because they are stuck in the past; they are making yesterday's or last week's trade in today's market. Yesterday they exited their positions too soon and left a lot of money on the table. So today, even though the market is acting very differently than it did yesterday, these traders try to hold their positions too long to get yesterday's profits from today's stingier market. Needless to say, it just does not work. Or, perhaps last week they sold the market at a certain price only to have the bulls rally just after their entry. They sustained a big loss. With cloudy vision they are concentrating on a market that is dead and gone. Today's market may be much weaker than the market last week and that losing trade from the past might be the perfect trade for today. But, traders that trade in the past cannot adapt; they are in a time warp. They remember yesterday's trade and in spite of the indicators, key numbers, and action of the market they pass up a winning opportunity. A successful trader must know where the market has been, but if you want to win, it is essential to trade in the present.

If my analysis tells me that just above or below a certain key number is a good entry point, I enter. Sometimes my timing is a little off or my stop is too tight and that trade is not profitable. When that happens, I keep my losses as low as I can and look for my next chance. I review the indicators and the factors that led me to make my decision in the first place. If I still believe that my analysis was correct, but my timing was slightly off, I reenter the market when that same opportunity presents itself again. The second time may be a charm and pay me big. Perhaps the two opportunities come minutes apart, hours apart, or days apart; it really does not matter. What matters is that if the market presents me with an opportunity that I have confidence in, I act.

Over the years I have observed a lot of my students trade. They have a great deal of difficulty trading in the present. After a loss it is hard for many of them to click that mouse again. They hesitate and the hesitation causes them to miss the best point of entry and give up some of their profits. Or, they just sit and watch as the market passes them by. Study the past and build on it, but you must always trade in the present.

HAVE A PLAN AND EXECUTE IT

With a clear understanding of the big picture and a workable view of the current market, you are ready to form your plan and execute. If you place a trade, be certain that you have identified your profit targets and your protective stop placement. Then, if the numbers tell you to buy or sell, have the courage to act. Click the mouse and get into the game. Sometimes it takes a lot of courage to trade. We all fear loss and defeat. But, if you have analyzed the situation carefully and know the extent of the risk that you are assuming, the fear should be minimized.

Once the trade is over, win or lose, move on to the next trading opportunity. The market will always present you with another chance. If you suffer losses, don't waste your time worrying about them. Learn from them and use them to improve your trading.

One of my students has all of the tools and skills to be successful. She is intelligent and understands how the markets work. Yet, she is not able to make money. She gets swallowed up by her losses. Until she learns to balance her emotions, she will not win.

KEEP A TRADING DIARY

Although you do not want to trade in the past or let historical events alter your analysis and judgment, you want to use former trading experiences to improve your trading skills. "If I could live my life again, I wouldn't change a thing." I have actually heard people say that. I can't understand that type of mentality. If I could live my 54 years over again, I would change a lot of things. Every single day would be better and better. I assure you that I would improve a tremendous amount the second time around. Unfortunately, we don't get a second chance, but if we use past experiences in a positive way and take the knowledge, insights, and lessons that we have learned from the past, we can use that information to create a better future.

Over the years I have read a great deal about the art of trading and about outstanding traders. Wall Street's brightest and best are a varied bunch of people. Each of them has a unique style and methodical twists. Some are long-term traders and others short-term. Some people trade equities and others focus on currencies, or options, or bonds, or some other vehicle. One great trader may use technical analysis while another relies on fundamentals. But, regardless of their approaches, they all do one thing and they all do it well; they continuously evaluate both their trading and the market. In this way they are able to adapt to changing conditions and constantly improve. The markets are dynamic and you must be too.

Record every trade that you make and the significant facts about it. What was your point of entry? Did the trade work for you? Where were your profit targets and how did you establish them? How large was your position? How did you execute the trade? Were there any problems, technical or otherwise? What market factors persuaded you to enter and exit the trade?

If the trade was a winner, did you maximize your profits or could you have made even more money by altering some of your techniques? If the trade was a loser, ask yourself why. Was your analysis correct or was it flawed? What logic or strategy led you to make the trade? What about your execution? Did you enter the trade at the opportune time or were you too slow or too fast? Consider your stops. Were they correctly placed? What about your profit targets, were they set too high or too low? Could you have exited a loser faster or let a winner run? Did you misread indicators? Did you use the correct type of order? In a highly volatile market a stop order can result in excessive slippage. Sometimes a stop-limit order can make or break the trade. Were you distracted and lacking focus? Did some external event like the news throw a monkey wrench into your plan? If so, should you have known about the news and been out of the market before it broke?

Write down the market conditions and the action you took in response. Then, analyze the hell out of it. If you could relive the experience, how would you act differently? What would you change and what would you keep the same? If you do not know what you did in the past you cannot correct yourself and learn from it. Therefore, it is highly probable that if you do not identify your mistakes you will repeat them in the future.

Successful traders do not accept mediocrity. They strive to understand why their winning trades were successful because they want to repeat them. Likewise, they have to comprehend what went wrong with the losers so that those mistakes can be avoided. Obviously, if we all limit our mistakes while enhancing and repeating our successes, our trading will improve and our bank accounts will grow. Just like the greats of Wall Street, you, too, have to always study, evaluate, and improve. If you do not, you won't be joining the Green Circle.

Don't Just Record Trades, Use the Past to Improve

My trading hero, Jesse Livermore, was a great believer in studying and evaluating his own trading. From his earliest trading days he kept a log and recorded information that he believed to be important. Then at night and during times away from the sweat shops and the trading office, he studied the information he had recorded. He used this information to identify patterns and trends and to critique his trading performance.

According to Richard Smitten, Livermore had a very unusual procedure for conducting his yearly analysis. At year's end, he packed a few necessities and went to the bank. He entered at the close of business on a Friday afternoon and walked quickly to the vault where his annual earnings of cash were stacked in piles on the floor. Once inside, the vault was locked and Livermore spent the weekend in solitude with his money and his notebook. He stayed in isolation for days going through his records and pondering his trades. He wanted to learn from his experiences and improve his trading for the upcoming year.

Livermore also liked to see his money and feel connected to it. He wanted to be reminded that the money was real. Sometimes as traders we start playing with numbers and we forget that we are playing with real money. Once that happens, we take risks that we should never take and act foolishly with our precious business capital. To stay in touch, Livermore believed in taking, spending, and enjoying some of the money he skillfully earned from Wall Street.

After he had finished his yearly analysis in the bank vault, he took a portion of his cash. He stuffed it into his pockets and his valise.

On Monday morning, the vault opened and he was ready to face another year with a clear perspective. With the profits he had taken from the vault, he began a shopping spree. He experienced the benefits of his trading in a very real and pleasurable way.

You don't have to lock yourself up in a bank vault to do your analysis. But, you have to do it somewhere. It is critical that you continuously evaluate and improve your skills.

Like Livermore, I also always keep a trading diary. I have done that for years. By sitting down at night and recording my trades, I identify my strengths and weaknesses. Once I become aware of them, I can prepare to avoid the mistakes while magnifying the strengths.

Set Realistic Goals

Never forget that trading is a business. Like any other business you must have realistic goals. What does trading success look like to you? Write your goals in your diary. On a daily basis, how will you achieve those goals? Every day, hold yourself accountable. Did you take a step toward the goal during your day's trading or did you move away from it?

Record your daily profit and loss totals. Remind yourself that the numbers are real and the money in your account was hard earned. Never separate yourself from the dollars in your account. Once you do, you are desensitized to your losses and they quickly get out of hand.

When you record your profit and loss totals daily and compare them with your profit-making goals, it may be enlightening. Say, for example, that you are a relative novice and you have set an average profit target of $50.00 a day. If you lose $50.00 on Monday, you have to make $100.00 on Tuesday to get back on target. If you lose $500.00 on Monday, it will take you ten winning days in a row to get back on target. That is the reason that you must keep losses low. Consistent large losses will devastate your account and close your trading business.

Beginning traders always have a tendency to take huge losses and tiny profits. Just be aware of that fact and work very hard on money management. By recording your profit and loss totals daily in your diary, you hold yourself accountable and you will be more inclined to work harder to preserve your capital.

Use Your Diary to Stay Disciplined

By recording your actions in a diary, you are also holding yourself accountable for following or not following your trading rules. For example, if you have decided that you will not trade during the news and you suffer a huge loss because you violated your rules, you have to face yourself. You have to write down the details in the diary and the evidence is there in black and white. You lost because you lacked discipline. Next time, you will remember that experience and be more conscious of the consequences of trading the news.

Or, perhaps you have told yourself that you will not trade more than three contracts until you are consistently profitable. But, you see an opportunity that seems to be pretty good. All of the indicators do not support a buy, but you quickly add up all of the profit you will make if you buy ten contracts and get four points of profit. Greed lures you into the market and you take a fantastic beating.

Record the whole ugly scene in the diary and hold your feet to the fire. Why did you not reach your goal on this date? You lost a lot of money because you did not have the discipline to follow your own rules. Write it down and acknowledge your mistake. Then ask yourself how you can improve tomorrow. The answer is obvious, follow your rules and exercise discipline.

In the diary you are the judge and the jury of your actions. Well, I guess that is not really quite right. The market has already rendered a verdict and meted out the punishment.

A friend and former student of mine, Ron, kept two diaries. He kept an emotional diary and a diary of key numbers. In this way, he was able to record the full array of his trading information and use it to improve.

REVISIT THE DIARY OFTEN

Don't just keep a diary, use the diary. Review it often and remind yourself of your good and bad business practices. Especially during times when your trading is off, get out the diary and review it. Within its pages there is probably the secret as to how you can stop the losses and turn them into wins.

And, don't just ponder the bad days and the bad trades. Study the winners too. See what you did well and pat yourself on the back for it. If you took profits at just the right point or selected a perfect entry level, congratulate yourself and try to repeat the experience over and over again.

Throughout your trading career, learn and improve so that your goals can be reached and your bank account fattened!

Get a Trading Buddy

Trading can be a lonely job. In your circle of friends and family, you may be the only trader. Try to find someone who understands what you do and the experiences that you have. I have many dear friends who are traders and I enjoy talking with them. When we, as traders, have a hard time, we need other traders who can talk with us and help us.

Many years ago I met a very fine trader, Linda Bradford Raschke. Over the years, when I have gone through difficult trading times, I have spoken to Linda and she has given an understanding and helpful ear. Often she had some advice for me, but even if she did not, just being able to talk with her helped to clear my thinking and improve my trading. I hope that I have also been able to help her from time to time.

My point is that we can all benefit from associating with and talking to other traders. We can help to support each other and hopefully through our relationships our trading will also be improved.

Do you remember the line from the movie, *The Right Stuff*: "Who is the best pilot you ever saw?" Well, I used to ask myself the question: "Who is the best trader you ever saw?" Often, I arrogantly thought that it was me. However, through my school I have met many interesting people who share my love of trading. Three of them are Virgil, Peter, and Debbie. Debbie helps me with my trading strategy. She often sees things that I may overlook. Today, when I ask myself, "Who is the best trader you have ever seen?" my answer is Debbie.

Virgil helps me with business ideas and offers creative suggestions. Peter encourages me with his persistence and determination. All of us have bad days and bad trades, but we have to keep our perspective and move on. Having a friend to share your experiences is priceless.

REVIEW

Trading is a profession. Just like any other profession, you need to get prepared and educated. Know all that you can about the markets and our financial landscape. In addition, on a daily basis, always be ready to trade. Don't trade until you have studied the day's market and know the key numbers. Identify support and resistance and be ready to take advantage of your knowledge when the time is right. Also be sure to know when scheduled economic reports will be aired so that you will not be caught off guard.

Keep a big picture of the market in your mind at all times and use that picture as a background to frame current market conditions. Without a big picture of the market in your mind, you will not be a very successful trader.

Always have a plan and execute the plan. When you click your mouse know where you will enter, take profits, and exit if the trade turns against you. Always know the risk involved with every trade.

Record all of your trades. Keep a detailed trading diary and study it. Use your past mistakes and successes to improve your trading. Learn from the past but always trade in the present. You cannot change yesterday's trade but you can benefit from it by using it as a springboard to greater profitability.

LESSONS LEARNED

- Be prepared to trade and take advantage of opportunities presented.
- Study the past but trade in the present.
- Record a detailed trading diary each and every day.
- Hold yourself accountable for violating your rules or not exercising discipline. Likewise, pat yourself on the back for following the rules.
- Visit your diary often and remind yourself of your strengths and limit your weaknesses.

CHAPTER 11

A Study in Contrast

June 1986, Oklahoma City. It is Monday and I arrive at the office early to review my accounts and get ready for trading. I want to be set to go the minute the market opens. No need to waste any time. I like my first trades to hit the floor minutes after the opening bell rings and do not plan to execute my last trade of the week until minutes, or even seconds, before the market closes on Friday.

Laura, my assistant is only minutes behind me. She is a dedicated employee who is always ready to help me accomplish my tasks. She checks the desk to be certain that our trading equipment is ready. Our equipment consists of our data feed, a telephone with a dedicated line that connects us directly to the trading floor, and a stack of order tickets. We both keep our eyes on the clock so that we will be seated and ready when the first trade of the week is made on the floor.

I sit at my desk and Laura sits opposite me. We are both watching the market numbers and she is listening intently for trading directions. At 8:30 A.M. Central Time, the bell rings and the game is on.

Immediately the market moves down and it looks like a sell-off. I respond, "Sell 15 S&Ps at the market."

Laura grabs the phone and delivers the order to the floor while she is rapidly jotting down the order on our tickets.

Ten minutes pass and the market shifts. My original 15 contracts are not profitable. The market is going higher. Now it has crossed its opening price and looks to be seeking even higher prices.

145

"Sell another 15 S&Ps at the market. Let's average down. This market is going down. I feel it," I say.

Again, Laura quickly follows my commands and executes the order.

It is only 8:50 A.M. and the market has been in session for 20 minutes, however, I decide to sell 15 more contracts. I have to keep on averaging down because the market is moving against me. If I just keep selling, when the market shifts, I can make my money back on those 30 contracts that I already executed.

"Sell 15 more S&P's at the market."

I see her lift the telephone and call the floor.

The tickets are beginning to stack up and it is only 9:00 A.M.

By 9:15 A.M., I am down thousands of dollars and I decide to buy. My arbitrage system consists of buying the S&P 100. These are index options that are traded on the OEX Exchange. I cover my 45 S&P 500 index future contracts and hold on and hope.

It's 10:00 A.M. and I still have not made money. I limited my losses but I decide to speed up my trading. I take my shorts in the S&P 500 Index to the market and flip to the long side. With every dip and upswing in the market, I am buying or selling. I am working both the S&P 500 Index Futures and the S&P 100 index options.

There is no time to stop and think about it or do any sort of analysis. That will slow us down. Just watch the market as it moves and react to it.

Lunchtime comes and goes, but Laura and I snack on whatever we can find that is in the office. We do not break for lunch. Coffee breaks—we don't take them. We can't miss any trading opportunities. If we absolutely must, we race to the bathroom. But, we make that trip as seldom as possible. We need to keep our eyes on the market.

Throughout the day we keep the telephone line hot and the pencils busy as we telephone in and write out orders. We make literally thousands of transactions. I am profitable one minute and down the next. My heart is pounding and sweat is pouring down my brow. Laura reaches for the aspirin. She has a pounding headache. I simultaneously grab a huge bottle of Tums. My stomach is flipping. I need to ease the ache because we have hours to go before we slay this dragon.

When the market closes and the orders finally cease, we are both exhausted. I think I made money, but I am really not quite certain. In the morning I'll get the confirmation tickets and the final tally.

My trading style resembles a gun slinger in the Old West. Load my gun and fire all the bullets as fast as I can. Then, reload and repeat. Follow the process over and over again. Hopefully, the barrage of bullets will hit the target and some of them will even land in the bull's eye.

Laura and I breathe a sigh of relief, complete our office tasks, and drag out of the office and head for home. Tomorrow, we will begin again. We work very hard and we believe that we are good traders because we concentrate on the market and take our trading very seriously.

June 2005, Mobile, Alabama. It's 9:00 A.M. on Saturday morning. I get a fresh cup of coffee and head for my easy chair; my feet go up and I get comfortable. My trading week is about to begin; or, at least my preparation for it. I always begin by watching the business news on Saturday. I need to know about major national and international events that may impact the financial markets. My favorite shows are broadcast by FOX. These shows recap the business developments of the past week and preview the important events that are anticipated during the upcoming week. I like to listen to this block of business information for topics that are of special interest to me. I do not look for details, but I want the broad overview. The shows that I watch begin at 9:00 A.M. and end at 11:00 A.M.

Enough media commentary—after two hours of watching the television and reflecting on the economic scene, I enjoy the remainder of my weekend. Play a little golf and enjoy some movie time. No more business until Sunday.

On Sunday, I like to read *Barrons*. I read selected articles and get a feel for the general tone of things. You may read the hard copy or subscribe on line. Or, you may prefer another publication. Over the years, I have found *Barrons* helpful. Some of the columns are very important to me. I always review the economic calendar. It is helpful because it reviews information about the past week's major reports and also previews scheduled news events for the upcoming week. I also like to read the *Trader* column. I find it interesting and somewhat helpful. After that, I read the headlines throughout the paper. If an article especially interests me, I read it. However, I do not read the paper word-for-word. Just like with the television news, I am not looking for a lot of details. I am looking for the big picture so that I can be well informed and ready for Monday.

Finally, I gather market numbers. I review the yearly opens; I look at the monthly opens and the weekly opens for all major futures indices and for other things that I plan to trade. I study charts from the former week and note how the markets and indices responded at certain price levels. I look and visualize what is going on. Finally, I look at the latest daily opens. I determine where the market is trading in relation to where it has been. I want to clearly understand the trading landscape. That way, when I see certain prices and scenarios, I am ready to respond. I have completed my analysis and I am not going to be a deer caught in the headlights. I know through this structure that whatever happened the previous week is erased and I am mentally ready for what the new week will bring.

I actually begin my first look at the real-time market numbers on Sunday afternoon. The S&P Index Futures opens at 5:00 P.M. I like to watch the open and note and record the opening price, but I do not begin trading. However, if I decide to trade, I do not need an assistant; I can just use the laptop in my office and click the mouse. I have my data feed on the laptop along with my charting programs and my trading platform.

After getting the information that I need, I walk away. No need to place a trade. The week is young and there will be plenty of opportunities to trade when I have a clearer view of where things are going. Now it's time to enjoy an early dinner or check the movie listings.

At 7:00 P.M., I again return to my computer. I am interested in how the market is trading in relation to its open. If there has been a deviation from the opening price that appears to be significant, I may place a trade. If the market looks too quiet and no direction is discernible, I walk away and enjoy the evening. I get a good night's rest in preparation for the trading week ahead.

THE WEEK BEGINS

It's 5:00 A.M. and I slip out of bed and walk to my office down the hall. I feel a little groggy, but the anticipation of looking at the market always wakes me up. I believe, just like the old adage, that the early bird catches the worm. In fact, I have a trade that I sometimes take that I call the Early Bird Trade. It is placed at 4:00 A.M. However, I do not always get up for that trade. I only take that trade if I get a telephone call from my son Morgan; and this morning I did not get the call so I caught an extra hour of sleep.

My Early Bird Trade has very specific criteria. It is only made if, at 3:30 A.M., the direction of the Asian markets, the European markets, and the U. S. markets all agree. For years, I got up early and checked these markets. However, when Morgan turned 16, he decided to start a little business and get up for me. For a small fee, he agreed to check everything out and wake me up only if the criteria had been met. I loved the idea so I gladly paid him each month for his services. A lot of my students loved the idea too, and Morgan developed a very lucrative business. He is now 22, and to this day he rises at 3:00 A.M., looks at the market, and if he sees a trend, he calls all of his customers and alerts them that a lucrative trade may be ripe for the picking. But, like I said, on this day I did not get the call and now it is 5:00 A.M.

In my office at home I have several monitors and my RoadMap software running. My program is busy continuously recording market data for me, as it always does. I look at the price of the S&P Futures, the Dow Futures, and the Nasdaq Futures. In fact, I review all of the markets and look for several things. First, I want to know how each market is trading in relation to its opening price. Is there significant deviation? Next, I want to know if the major futures markets are all moving in the same direction or not. In other words, is there consistency among the markets? Does there seem to be a general consensus that the bulls or the bears are dominant? If so, I might want to start paying more attention. If there is clearly divergence among the major futures markets, I know that I am not interested in trading until they decide to agree. I step away and wait.

At 6:00 A.M., it's time to put my toe in the water. I go back to the computer screen. My special concern is the DAX Futures. I note and record the 6:00 A.M. price because that number is a major pivot number. I use that pivot number in conjunction with the other information that I have gathered to begin trading. If the DAX is trading above its 6:00 A.M. pivot, I will be looking to the long side. If it is trading down from the 6:00 A.M. price, I will be looking to the short side. I often place a trade during this time. Unless, that is, there is scheduled news coming out soon.

I know and understand the significance of news. If there is some report being aired, I take small profits. I am content with those little gains for the time being because news makes the market too dangerous for a long-term play. I do not want to take the added risk of staying in the market and going for big profits. I will have other chances to ride the waves, but now I want to control risk.

If there is no news expected, I trade early in an attempt to take some quick profits and position myself for a free ride. That is, I want to take enough fast profits out of the market to be able to keep a small position riding. I use my Three Ts approach to accomplish this. I put on a position and hope to exit two-thirds to three-fourths of it quickly and profitably. Then, I can move my stop to break even and ride. If a trend is developing, it will likely accelerate as New Yorkers wake up and see it. They will join the move and add to its strength-all the better for me.

If I succeed in my early play, my downside will be covered. Once I get into a free-ride position, there is no fear and no risk for me. I am working with the market's money and I am able to relax and enjoy playing the game.

You do not get a free ride every day. It may only happen once a week or so. But, when you get that ride, it is sweet. If the market is especially opinionated and decides to make a major move in one direction or another, you can just sit and glide it like a surfer catching one of those huge Hawaiian waves. It is thrilling and if you play it correctly, you can make your weekly income during that one day. Even if you make the play and things don't work out, if you have exited a large part of your position with some profit, even if small, you should be okay. Many times, I make money even when the trade does not work out like I planned. The trick is to pick the right entry prices at the right times and take some quick profits. Then, move your stop to break even. After that, it's all gravy. Sometimes you get a much larger payback than at other times. Just consistently keep losses low. That is the big secret to trading and, of course, it is the hardest part.

Trading in the open pits begins on the S&P Index Futures at 8:30 A.M. As any experienced trader knows, it is a volatile time for the market. There is a lot of jumpy action and it is easy to lose money fast. Therefore, I am generally out of most of my early morning positions by this time. Unless, that is, I have been on the winning team long enough to be trading with the market's money.

Far more often than not, I am not in the market when the pits open and I do not enter any market until I watch it trade for a while. However, I use this time to gather information and identify key numbers. I want the information noted on my daily worksheet and I want to identify support and resistance levels. I look at 30-minute bar charts and my reference bars to get this information.

Be cautious with your first trade of the day. It is so easy to get excited and enter before the time is right. If you lose on your first trade, it gets you behind the eight ball. I try to keep my losses in the early morning to a bare minimum. Only lose one tenth of your daily tilt balance during this time. You want to start profitably so you don't spend your day doing catch up. Also, if you are down from the beginning, your judgment may be easily impaired and it is easy to lose more money by trying to make up for the loss that you have already incurred. Therefore, don't let that mouse finger get itchy. Remember that you do not have to trade until you are ready and until the market gives you a clear signal of its intentions. Many times, the wisest decision a trader can make is to sit still and enjoy being a spectator.

If I see a trade between 9:00 and 9:15 A.M., I take it. But if I am not in the market by 9:15, I do not place a trade until 9:30 A.M. I like to get market readings on the half hours. Generally, if I am not in the market by 15 minutes after the hour, I wait for the next 30-minute reading.

I follow the market closely until about 10:15 A.M. Hopefully, the market was good and I made some money. However, if I have not executed a trade, it is fine because I still have plenty of time before the market closes.

I often eat with my students. I have no interest in the market until 12:30 P.M. At that time, I want to know the S&P price because it is a very important pivot number for the rest of the day.

I watch the S&P Index Futures very carefully between 12:30 and 1:15 P.M. The market often shows its hand after lunch and I want to identify its direction. If I see a trend developing, I trade. If no trend is discernible, I wait until 2:30 P.M.

I do not trade from 1:30 to 2:30 P.M. because the market tends to be slow and difficult to read during this time. I get away from the trading platform and entertain myself elsewhere. I make a few telephone calls, talk to the folks in the office, and think.

At 2:30 P.M., I come back to the computer and get ready for the close of the session. I review the numbers. As the closing minutes approach, the market does not necessarily follow its daily pattern. It may move in a contrary position. If there are a lot of shorts in the market, the big boys may move things up and squeeze out the sellers into the close. For that reason, I look at the 2:30 P.M. price and note the volume and movement. If I see a pattern, I jump on board. Sometimes, this is a very lucrative play.

LET THE NUMBERS LEAD THE WAY

Although I follow the detailed schedule, that does not mean that if an exceptional opportunity presents itself, I will not take it. If Osama is captured on a Sunday afternoon you can be sure that I will be at my computer. I will be buying the market. By the time the opening bell officially rings on Monday, less educated traders will be buying it from me, and I will be taking my money to the bank.

Some of my students are very successful and they do not follow my schedule; they create their own that adapts to their specific needs. For example, my son Winston is a trader. He just graduated from college and has been trading for years. All through college he earned his spending money by trading the DAX Futures on Friday mornings. Monday through Thursday, he slept late. But, when Friday arrived, he got out of bed early and went to work. His system worked and he was able to accomplish his goal by focusing on that one market and by trading one day out of the week.

Computers and the internet offer us a great opportunity. As traders, we now have so much more data and the ability to trade whenever we see a good money making set-up.

COUNTING MY CASH OR MOURNING MY LOSS

After the market closes, I find a quiet spot and reflect. I review the day and consider the current character of the market. Was it choppy, trending, or volatile? How was my trading? I look at all of my trades—good and bad—and I evaluate them. I want to learn all that I can because when the night market opens, I may well be a player.

The S&P Globex market opens at 3:30 P.M. (the Sunday open is 5:00 P.M.) and I will record and study those numbers. Just like the night before, I will keep abreast of market developments and be ready to play if I see a winning hand. But, I will not rush to the market on a whim. Before I trade, I analyze and formulate a strategy so that the odds will be in my favor and the risks will be minimized.

REVIEW

Years ago, trading was very different in a lot of respects. First, the method of executing orders was not electronic. Orders were telephoned into the trading floor. I had no laptop for researching information and getting into and out of markets easily. Aside from this obvious difference, I was different. I spent about 90 percent of my trading day placing orders and only about 10 percent of my time thinking about the market. I did very little analysis. I reacted to the numbers that Wall Street was giving me and I hoped that by making literally thousands of trades that I would make money.

When each weekday ended, I was spent. I did not take a lunch break. I did not take coffee breaks. I rarely left my desk. I remember one day when I had to go to the bathroom. I did not have a stop in place and when I came back to my desk, my account was down $20,000.00. I lost $20,000.00 while I was in the bathroom. Every time I got on the elevator when the market was in session, I was tense and worried. How would the market move while I was in the elevator? Would my account be up or down when I arrived at my floor?

I always thought I was prepared. I took my job seriously and I worked to be well informed. In fact, I worked incredibly hard. But in 1986 my preparation was far different than it is in 2005.

Now, I use the weekends to prepare. I check media coverage of business and financial news and take note of significant occurrences. I can use my computer to research and analyze while I am at home. With the help of charts and my records, I identify support and resistance levels and plan for the week ahead. When the markets open on Sunday afternoon, I am ready. I have formulated a strategy and am ready to execute it if and when the chance presents itself.

Today, my focus is shifted. I spend about 90 percent of my time thinking and analyzing and only about 10 percent trading. I appreciate and understand the significance of planning and preparation. I may not trade continuously, but my software collects market data continuously. I am able to check the numbers and find the trends. My trading is not hectic. It is calculated and concentrated. As I noted in the beginning of the book, I do not trade for the fun or excitement of the trade. I trade to make money. Interestingly, I make more money because I don't waste my bullets. No more gun slinging. I take calculated aim.

LESSONS LEARNED

- Use the weekend to get informed about financial events.
- Study charts of the past week's trading and identify key numbers that may be reached in the week ahead.
- Learn about upcoming scheduled news events.
- Visualize the big picture of the market.
- Plan a weekly strategy. Get ready to take calculated aim.

CHAPTER 12

Recap the Essentials

T rading requires the mastery of a number of skills including market analysis and tape reading, execution, emotional balance, and, especially, money management. A trader can achieve a high level of proficiency in one or more of these skills, but that is not enough. A trader has to be good at all of them. Furthermore, it is not sufficient that the skills are mastered in isolation. The winning trader must integrate them into a daily routine and get them all working together. Such mastery is not easy and it is not attained overnight; but with dedication and many hours of hard work, the art of trading can be mastered and the successful student can join the winner's circle.

Several years ago someone at DTI came up with an idea that has helped many of my students. If we are profitable at the end of the day, even if we are only profitable by one dollar, we put a green circle on our calendar. We work very hard to stay in what we call Green Circle Country. This may sound silly but it helps us to remember our goal and hold ourselves accountable. No one enjoys looking at his or her calendar and seeing a lot of red days. On the other hand, we take great pride in our rows of green circles.

This chapter is a review of the materials presented. Hopefully, it will help you to synthesize the information and understand how it all fits together so that you can join the winners in Green Circle Country.

BEGIN WITH TIME

Trading is time sensitive; there are some hours and time segments during the day when the chances of success, at least with my method, are generally best. There are other times when a wise trader will usually stay out of the market and be a spectator. The good times are those times with greatest liquidity and volatility; I designated these times as trade zones because these are the times that I believe my chances of success are best. I have three zones during each trading day. The times are as follows: 9:00 to 10:15 A.M., 12:00 to 1:15 P.M., and 2:15 to 2:45 P.M. These generally active markets offer the opportunity for me to use my Three T's of Trading approach and they also make reading the tape easier for me because the markets tend to be more predictable when there is activity. If the market gets too quiet and the volume falls off dramatically, the indicators are less reliable and you may have to keep a position open for too long without getting paid. While you are just sitting in a stale, slow market, a heavy player can step in and artificially move prices, resulting in a losing position for you. Therefore, you do not want to buy or sell and just sit and wait; a quick turn in the market could catch you like a deer in the headlights. Just like the scene at a deer-car collision, it would probably not be a pretty sight.

In addition to these generally ideal trading times, there are also some times when you want to stay out of the markets. Between 1:30 and 2:15 P.M., there is often a countertrend and even well-placed protective stops can be hit. I refer to this time as the Grim Reaper and I keep my hands away from my mouse. Also, if I trade between 12:30 and 1:00 P.M., I am always a buyer. That is the case because during this 30-minute period, the market often gives off false signals; it may appear to be selling off, but more often than not, by 1:00 P.M. it finally decides to move up, even if just slightly. Therefore, during this time I either buy or stay out of the market. I lost money too many times by shorting the market during this time.

Know How Markets Are Trading Around the Clock and Around the Globe

The United States is only one nation among many and likewise U.S. markets are not the do all and be all of the financial world. After U.S. day sessions end, night sessions open in New York and Chicago and day sessions open in Asia and Europe while Americans are sleeping. The most active markets tend to be the markets in the countries where the sun is shining. Some of the largest United States companies are traded on foreign exchanges. Therefore, knowing how the Nikkei (Tokyo), Hang Seng (Hong Kong), DAX (German), FTSE (London), CAC (French), and other markets are trading can give us insight into how our markets are doing around the globe. It can also give us some idea of the strength or weakness of some of the other powerful economic forces around the world. By having this information, I think I have an edge on traders that do not have it. When the markets in Chicago and New York open for their daily trading sessions, I feel as though I have a little more information than the average person because I did a little more homework and have an idea about what is going on in major foreign markets.

The German DAX is a big index and I both trade it during the early morning hours, and I use it as a market indicator. It is part of my tape reading process. As long as it is open, it is one of the gauges that I use to determine market direction. Is it bullish or bearish? Does it agree or disagree with the Dow, Nasdaq, and S&P Futures?

The bottom line is that I use a 24-hour trading clock to gain a market edge. I do not stay up all night; I have software that records and charts the information that I need.

Yearly Times Are also Very Important

The single most significant market data that I gather every year is the opening prices for the markets, indices, commodities, and stocks that I plan to trade during the course of the year. I then use that information to begin forming a monthly and weekly trend line. By always knowing the direction of my line and its distance away from its opening price, I am able to determine whether the market's big picture trend is bullish or bearish. Having this information helps me to stay on the right side of the market and avoid the pitfalls of false and momentary market moves that the big boys may make in an attempt to take my money.

Pay Attention to Holidays

New Year's Day is not the only date that a savvy trader needs to watch. There are other dates that the market seems to use as benchmark spots to review and reassess itself. These noteworthy dates include April 15, Memorial Day, July 4, Labor Day, Thanksgiving, and Christmas.

In fact, the entire month of December is a fantastic time for my trading. The holiday spirit often begins in the market in late November and continues until the big New Year's celebration in Times Square. December is not always an up month, but in my experience, it is a very financially lucrative time for me to trade and I love it.

Timeout Helps Break a Losing Streak

Everybody has losing times during their trading. Sometimes we may have difficulty for just a day or two; while other times may last for days or even weeks. One of the ways a trader can break a losing streak is to take some time off. Rest, clear your mind, and try to analyze your mistakes. How can you alter your trading to turn your losers into winners? During this time off, if you trade, do simulations or paper trade. Don't put your money at risk until you have identified and corrected the problem.

INTEGRATE NUMBERS WITH TIME

Every market, exchange, index, commodity, and stock respects some price points more than others. These honored points tend to be pivotal areas where support and resistance are exerted. There are two types of key numbers: historical key numbers and numbers that have flexed their muscles in recent trading. For a list of historical numbers, you may want to glance back at Chapter 3. However, the list provided is not all inclusive. The best way to identify key numbers is through observation and study over time.

Other key numbers rise to the surface as the markets trade. For example, as the markets moves downward, buyers step in at certain points and offer support; and as the markets move upward, sellers step in at other points to try to hold it down. These support and resistance price points are key numbers. If you want to be a winner, you need to know them. By having this knowledge, you will be less apt to buy the highs and sell the lows. You will know that you do not want to buy just below a major point of resistance and you do not want to sell just above support. Support and resistance need to be broken before you put your money at risk.

Use Key Numbers for Entry, Exit, and Stops

I use key numbers in several ways. First, I use the yearly, monthly, and weekly opening price to create a trend line that depicts the big market picture. Once I have a broad view of the markets, I am better able to analyze current market moves and decide whether I should be long, short, or out of the market altogether. When the market opens every day, I have that big picture in my mind and it helps me to stay on the right side of the market.

Once I have a clear long-term view, I focus on shorter and shorter time periods and zero in on the trade at hand. I identify the key numbers that are nearest to the point where the market is currently trading. Then, I use those key numbers to determine entry points, profit targets, and stop placement.

If I am buying the market, I do not want to buy it just below a major key resistance point. Such an action would be foolish. Instead, I want my point of entry to be just above resistance so that I can ride the market up to the next resistance point and make money.

Likewise, I do not want to sell just in front of support. If the bulls are too strong and the bears too weak, the support will hold and I will be in a losing situation. Knowing and wisely using key numbers helps me to make money. I cannot emphasize enough the value of key numbers. If you are not familiar with key numbers and do not use these numbers in your trading, I strongly suggest that you refer back to Chapter 3 because key numbers are unquestionably very important.

READING THE TAPE IS THE SKILL OF MARKET ANALYSIS—LEARN IT

Accurate tape reading is essential for successful trading. Without it, a trader is like a hiker lost in a dense forest with no compass and does not know where to go. There are a lot of aspects to tape reading. First, you need a big picture view of the broad market so that you are aware of the markets general tendency. Is Wall Street singing a bullish or a bearish tune?

After you have a clear concept of the big picture, focus down to the current market. Compare the immediate trading situation to the big picture trend. Are they in agreement? If not, how far apart are they? If the big picture is strongly bullish and the current market is slightly bearish, be cautious of selling. The market may just be experiencing a dip and the bull may quickly return to gore you. By using key numbers and trend lines, you can, hopefully, stay on the winning side.

Once you have a big or long-term market view as well as a current or short-term view, verify your analysis. Do other indicators and market support your opinion?

Check Other Markets

Major market, indices, and exchanges tend to trend together. I always track the S&P Futures Index, the Dow Futures, the DAX Futures, and the Nasdaq Futures. Before deciding to enter the market, I look for confirmation from these other markets. Say, for example, that I am considering buying the S&P Futures, before I buy I want to know if these other markets are also bullish. If the bulls are in charge of the other markets, I feel that my buying action has confirmation. However, if there is divergence in the market, I step aside and look closer. Sometimes when a major index or exchange is lagging, there is a reason for it. Do not ignore it. Instead, use it like a red flag of caution and dig deeper and look harder at the market. I have often been saved from losing positions by seeing divergence among the markets and staying out. If there is a genuine bullish or bearish move, the big indices and exchanges will generally all join in and move in the same direction, thus, offering you confirmation of your analysis or leading you to question your decision.

Never Read Prices in Isolation

Do not read prices in isolation. A price has no meaning unless it is placed in the context of the market. When placed in context, what does the price tell you? Is it a good buy or sell point? If not, stay away. Wait until you see the right set up for trading.

Before Clicking the Mouse, Be Sure That the Major Indicators Support You

There are a number of market indicators that can help you to read the tape. I always monitor the NYSE Issues, the Nasdaq Issues, the TICK, TRIN, V-Factor, and TTICK. Through years of experience and trading, I learned how to read and interpret these indicators. Chapter 4 explains them in depth and gives you direction as to how I use each one of them. Suffice it to say here that you need to check with all of them before trading and you need to have confirmation for your buying or selling position.

Time Is Another Aspect of Tape Reading

In order to read the tape correctly, you have to be aware of time and know the role that time plays in trading. A market indicator may mean one thing at 9:00 A.M., but the identical reading on that indicator may have a different meaning at 1:45 P.M. This is true because certain times during the day are more active than others and I find the market indicators easier to read and more reliable during the active times. When the market is too slow and there is a lull in the action, the indicators are less predictable and it is too easy to get false readings. Therefore, I generally stay out of the market during these times. My best trading opportunities present themselves during trade zones. Just be sure that when you are reading the tape, you are considering time and its significance.

Trading Is an Art and Not a Science

Always remember that trading is an art and not a science. There is no simple rule to follow that will always give you an ensured result. There are many shades of gray. Therefore, you need to dedicate yourself to the task of mastering tape reading. It is not easy and the skill is not developed overnight. Becoming a good tape reader can take hours, and maybe years, of devoted work and it will probably cost you more than a few dollars. But, if you are consistent and persistent, you can master this aspect of the trading game.

GOOD TRADING REQUIRES EMOTIONAL BALANCE

Every trader knows the power of emotions in trading. Once real money is put on the line, there is a tendency to get greedy, fearful, or act arrogantly. To be a winner, you must control these emotions and maintain balance.

Greed is a tremendously powerful emotion. It does not matter how much money we have, we always seem to want more. One of the most common misunderstandings of new traders is that they believe that they will begin day trading and get rich quick. I have never seen that happen. You must keep your expectations reasonable and in line with your level of training and experience. If you do not, you will be doomed to fail. Greed will cause you to enter trades that are too risky and you will lose money. Or, you will have a winning trade, but greed causes you to hold out for excessive profits that the market is unwilling to give you. Consequently, while you are waiting for that pot of gold at the end of the rainbow, the market hits a key number, shifts, and your profit turns into a loss. Keep greed in check or it will destroy your trading business.

Another dangerous emotion is fear. Trading involves calculated risks. If you are fearful of all risks, you cannot trade. That does not mean that you should act foolishly with your money and get yourself into dangerous situations where the odds are against you. What it does mean is that if you have analyzed the market carefully, determined the extent of your risk, know that you can afford the risk, and are willing to take it, relax and let your strategy work. Don't let fear sabotage trading. If you are overly fearful you will have trouble clicking the mouse even when market conditions are ideal and your analysis is perfect, you will hesitate, wait, and miss money making chances.

Fear will also destroy you in another way. It will make you question yourself every time the market moves even slightly against you. You may logically expect the market to dip or swing a little here and there. But, if fear takes charge, any move against your position makes you run for cover and exit what might be a winning trade. Generally when this happens, a loss is suffered when a profit could have been gained. Fear steals the rewards that could be attained if emotions are balanced.

A final emotion that often leads to extreme distress is arrogance. Many traders just can't seem to admit that they are wrong. They get into the market on the wrong side and then they ignore all of the indicators that are telling them of their mistake. They just keep deluding themselves into believing that they are right and the market will prove them to be so at any moment. In the meantime, their capital is eroding. Have faith in your analysis but do not be arrogant. Everyone makes mistakes. Study the market before you enter and identify the point at which you are sure that you are wrong. If the market goes to the identified point, exit your position and move to the sidelines for further analysis. Don't stay in the position and get slaughtered. Even the best traders make mistakes. Just try to keep your losses low so that you will be able to stay in the game for the long haul.

Some Techniques for Taming Your Emotions

I have several techniques that help me to stay in balance. First, I never trade without a protective stop. This is so important for a number of reasons. First, it saves you from a devastating loss if some news breaks or the market crashes or soars. Second, if you are wrong and you place your protection at the point that you know you are wrong, the market will hit your stop and gently remove you from the losing position. Without a hard stop in place it is too easy to stick with a losing position in the hopes that the market with shift. Hoping, wishing, and dreaming will not move or change the numbers. Just get out of losers as soon as you can and preserve your capital.

Another technique that I use is the two-minute rule. Most of my winning trades begin to pay me fast. My trading method is based on getting paid early and getting into a free-ride position. Therefore, I often watch the clock. If I am not in a profitable position within two minutes, I scrutinize the trade carefully. Perhaps I made a mistake and need to exit the position rather than accept a big loss. If the market is acting unpredictably, I do not want to be in it. So what if you exit the position and a few minutes later the market moves in your direction. You can always reenter the market. Just be sure that you focus on preserving your capital so that you can maintain your trading business.

ESTABLISH STRATEGIC OBJECTIVES AND BE TACTICAL

Traders that do not have a proven strategy are lost. They have no plan that can help them win the game. Their trading is no more accurate than the aim of an inexperienced and blindfolded gunman who fires at a target in the dark. Trading is a business and just like any other business, you need a strategic plan. Carefully analyze your personal financial situation and determine the amount of capital that you can risk on the venture. Think about yourself and your disposition. Can you deal with the potential losses that you may incur? Can you cope with the ups and downs of the market? Do you have the time to trade? If you want to master the game, you must invest not only money but time. You have to study, research, observe, and immerse yourself in the markets and data about them. If you don't have the money, the emotional predisposition, and the time to run and manage your trading, maybe you should select a different line of business.

If you have these assets and are willing to devote them to trading, then begin your study and devise an action strategy. There is one big market question that you must always answer before clicking your mouse and executing a trade: Should I be long, short, or out of the market? The answer to the question will guide your actions. Just be sure that when you answer the question your decision is confirmed by other markets, indices, and indicators.

The Three Ts of Trading Can Help You to Stay Profitable

I use a multiple contract trading approach. That is why I select my market entries so carefully. If I am not on target and do not manage my trade, I can lose more money than I could if I only traded one or two contracts. But, if I am accurate and manage effectively, I limit losses and increase profits. *(Remember that I have many years of experience. Beginners should start slowly and get profitable before trading large numbers of contracts. They should trade one or two contracts and hone their skills before attempting to trade multiples! Always consider risk first. For beginners, trading a large number of contracts is too risky.)*

Here are the basics of my approach: I buy or sell multiple contracts or equities and exit them at different levels of profitability. I use a portion of my positions to take quick profits. I call this the tick portion of the trade. After I get a few ticks in my favor, I lighten my load and put some money in the bank. Then, I aim for a second profit target and liquidate more of my position with more profit. This part of my approach is referred to as the trading portion. If I am trading the S&P Futures Index, I may be able to get two or three points of profit out of these positions. Finally, I follow the trend with the remaining contracts. This is, obviously, the trend phase, the final step in the trade.

By this time, if the trade has been successful, I have put money in the bank and I can move my stop to a break even position. Now I have limited my risk with the trade because the money I have already taken from the market will finance the trade for me. I refer to this strategy as getting a free ride from the market.

I use the Three Ts of Trading approach because it works for me. You may want to devise your own strategy. Be sure that it is a proven strategy that works for you. There are many ways to approach the market. Find one. Everyone is not comfortable with my strategy and I am not advocating that everyone adopt it. Every trader must take responsibility for his trading and be willing to accept the consequences of it. The big idea is that you have to have a proven strategy to win and if mine does not work for you, just find one that does.

A Strategy Must Be Tactically Executed

Once you have devised and mastered a proven strategy, you must execute it correctly. Watch time, key numbers, and market indicators. Don't hesitate when the time is right and don't jump in too early. Be consistent, disciplined, and prepared.

TRADING IS A BUSINESS THAT REQUIRES GOOD MONEY MANAGEMENT

Money management is an essential aspect of trading. One of the most common mistakes that beginners make is not managing their accounts. They lose too much money too fast and before they know it, their trading business is closing because their capital is gone. That is why it is so important to manage your trades and limit your losses.

Begin by managing your account balance. Determine the amount of money that you can afford to lose and that you can emotionally accept losing. Then, set that number as your tilt number. If you lose more than that amount on any trade or during any trading day, call it quits and close the trading platform. I cannot set your tilt number for you. You have to determine it for yourself based on your personality and your financial situation. Some traders use a 2 percent rule; whereas others risk more or less.

Another technique that I use is the three strikes and you are out rule. Regardless of my monetary loss, if I place three losing trades, I quit for the day. Clearly, something is not working for me and I need to stop and regroup. I quit even if my monetary loss is very small. Perhaps I managed the losing trades well and was able to get out of them before I lost my shirt. That does not matter. If I was wrong three times either the market is acting up or my analysis is just off. I accept that fact and head for the golf course.

I always know the risk involved with a trade before I take it. If the risk is too great and I cannot afford it or am unwilling to accept it, I just walk away. I let the trade go and wait for a better opportunity. Before I get into the market I identify my points of entry, my profit targets, and my stop placement. If my stop is hit, I accept my loss and wait for another chance.

I also manage every trade and try to limit my losses. It is easy to say and hard to do but work diligently to keep losses small and profits high. When you are in a trade keep your eyes on other markets and other indicators and continuously read the tape and adjust your strategy accordingly.

One of the most basic and critical ways to protect your capital is to trade with stops. At DTI we always teach traders to use stops. Without a protective stop you are totally at the mercy of market forces. If a disaster occurs you have no protection. It is true that if there is a dramatic and sudden market turn your stop may be passed over and you may not be taken out of the market. But, that would be the exceptional occurrence. If you have stops in place you have acted prudently to limit your loss in case of disaster. It worked for me and my students on September 11th. Our stop kept us from riding the market down.

Remember that trading is not a get rich quick game. Keep your greed in check by setting realistic goals and taking reasonable profits. If you experience a losing streak, take a timeout. Stop and analyze. Trade only a small position and identify and correct your error before you destroy your account balance.

NEWS CAN DESTROY THE PERFECT STRATEGY

Even if you have studied hard and have devised a winning strategy, there is one external force that can destroy you. That force is news. There are two types of news: breaking news and regularly scheduled economic reports. Breaking news cannot be controlled. A terrorist attack or some other devastating event can occur at any moment. All you can do to prepare is to always have protective stops in place and respond as quickly as possible to such an adverse event.

Regularly scheduled news events are quite different from breaking news. The public knows when the events are airing. We can read *Barrons*, *The Wall Street Journal*, or some other financial publication or we can check a host of web sites that provide this type of helpful information. My recommendation is to exercise extreme caution when scheduled news is reported. The markets often respond to such news in an extremely irrational and dramatic fashion. You don't want to be caught off guard in that type of situation. Unless you are very experienced and really know what you are doing you should never be in the market when economic news is being reported. Liquidate your positions and move to the sidelines. Let the news come out and let the market digest it. Only then should you consider trading.

Chapter 8 contains some of the most important market moving reports, but there are many others. Before you begin your trading day be sure that you know the financial and economic reports that will be published that day and plan your trading accordingly. If you are not informed and do not realize that a market move is based on news, you may foolishly enter a position only to find out that you have bought the high or sold the low. Don't be in that situation. Be informed and be out of the market before the news breaks.

A WINNING TRADER HAS TO GET THE RIGHT EQUIPMENT

Technology has come a long way in the last several decades and trading has been greatly altered by these changes. Today it is imperative that traders have the right equipment and get the right data and information if they want to be successful. Therefore, in Appendix B, I discussed some of the basic equipment and other things that you will need to begin trading online. Because technological advances are continuously being made, this information will be outdated over time. However, it may be helpful to some of you who are just beginning to play the game. The big idea is that you have to have the right equipment or your chances of success will be diminished.

ALWAYS PREPARE, EVALUATE, AND IMPROVE

Every professional knows the value of continuing to improve the skills of the job. The professional knows that it is important to stay up to date. Trading is no different than any other profession. If you want to stay at the top of your game, you, too, have to continue to learn and critique yourself.

Of course you want to read, study, observe, and learn as much as you can from other professionals and from the market itself. But, one of your best sources of information is your own trading. Keep a trading diary and use it. Record the trades you make and the reasons you made them. Study both your winners and your losers and learn from them. How can you reduce losses? How can you increase profits? Your trading log contains the answers. Study it carefully.

Once you identify your mistakes, correct them. Don't just repeat the same errors day after day. If you are continuously making losing trades, you must learn why and fix it. Otherwise, your trading business will end before it has a chance to really get off the ground.

As I noted at the beginning of this review chapter, trading is hard. If you are a beginner, approach the markets slowly and only trade after you have identified and tested a proven strategy. Then hone your skills and take small steps. When you begin, trade only one or two contracts and make sure that you are profitable before you increase your positions. Be smart and prepare well before trading.

The crash of 1987 taught me to manage risk first and consider profits second. If you discipline yourself to always do that, you will be far better off and your chances of success will be tremendously enhanced.

Throughout this book I shared some of the events that impacted my trading and my life. The stories are simple but the lessons in them are far bigger than the stories themselves. These lessons have helped both me and my students. Remember that every day is a new day and a new opportunity. Learn from the past. Live in the present. Get ready for the future. The market will crash again. Be prepared.

Good luck with your trading!

CHAPTER 13

An Afterthought for Consideration

The Doctrine of Genius

Many people think that you need to be a genius to beat Wall Street. I call this theory the Doctrine of Genius. There was a time when I, too, accepted this principle. However, today, after having observed numerous students for almost ten years, I hold a different view.

I have known a lot of very smart people in my lifetime; people that I consider to be geniuses. Geniuses come in different varieties. Some of them excel in technology. They have a gift for designing and building some of the very best widgets on the market. Others geniuses are doctors or lawyers. Their analytical skills are exceptional and if they are on your case, either in the emergency room or the courtroom, you know that you have the best. Still others geniuses are computer geeks. They understand absolutely, positively everything about computers, but they might have a great deal of difficulty discussing an episode of *Friends* or engaging fellow workers in idle chat at the water cooler.

By definition, geniuses are smarter than the rest of us. Their light bulbs in the crania just glow a little brighter. While the average person is operating with 100 watts or so, these folks are enjoying the extra illumination of 200 watts or more. Geniuses are really bright and, as a rule, they know it.

But, does that mean that they are good traders? For years I presumed that exceptionally intelligent people would naturally learn the rules of the game quickly and use their brilliance to gain wealth in record breaking speed. However, over the years, I have learned that the Doctrine of Genius principle is seriously flawed. Having a high IQ, without other skills and characteristics, does not make a Wall Street winner.

Why does the Doctrine of Genius prove to be untrue? I have given the question a lot of thought and I think that there are a number of reasons. I explain some of the reasons as follows.

First, the real engine behind the financial market is average people. They are the buyers and the sellers in the market. Millions and millions of these 100 to 120 or so IQ people from across the United States and around the world buy and sell stocks. The problem is that the genius types just do not think like most; consequently, their market analyses are also different. Their analyses do not always translate into wiser choices.

For example, a genius man might fall in love with a new company that produces some computer innovation. The man sees the value of the product and believes that the world will embrace it. He invests his entire portfolio in it. However, there just are not enough geniuses out there and the market share for the company is too small. The company goes belly up. Had the genius thought like the rest of us, he might have realized that the product was interesting, but that there was no mass market for it.

Now take the average person. She uses a household product every day and likes it. She has a chance to invest in the company that produces it and invests big. Across the population, there are so many of these average people that agree with her and like the product that it sells like hot cakes. The company grows by leaps and bounds and she pockets a lot of money. Sometimes it helps to be just an average person.

Second, geniuses have problems with admitting mistakes. In fact, they can have trouble with even seeing their mistakes because they are not accustomed to making them. In school, they were generally right. They were the people always making the A++ while the rest of us were making the Bs and Cs. They just can't seem to deal with errors. "A mistake? Surely not by me!"

When the geniuses analyze the market and make a decision; of course, they think that their decision is right. But what if they are wrong? In contrast, I know that I might be wrong. I am always watching the market indicators and the other indices and exchanges so that I can confirm or disprove my original opinion of market direction. Geniuses react differently when it comes to questioning themselves because they are so sure that they are right. As the market goes against a genius investor, the investor doesn't react appropriately because of this inability. Soon, a genius investor's account is empty.

Trading involves making mistakes. No trader is right all of the time. In fact, you do not have to be right all of the time to be a very successful trader. However, you need to be right more times than you are wrong and you need to do a good job of risk management. This situation is where realizing your mistakes and correcting them is essential. If traders do not realize that they have made a mistake and exit losing positions quickly, they will not be in the game very long. A few really bad trades and they are out of money and playing Scrabble or Monopoly instead of Wall Street's greatest game with you and me.

Third, geniuses are often too analytical. The markets move quickly. Another problem that highly intellectual people seem to have is a penchant for deep thinking and analysis. The market is a rapidly moving institution. But the genius is analyzing everything and cannot make a decision. The problem is that while a genius trader is conducting a very precise and detailed analysis, the market is moving like a bolt of lightening across a stormy sky.

You do not have time to write a doctoral thesis before you click the mouse. You must be prepared but that preparation should be been done well in advance of the market move. When the day begins, a good trader is ready and has recorded all of the needed data. A good trader has a big picture of the market in view at all times, and clearly sees how the current market fits into that picture. A good trader has identified the key numbers and if the time is right to put money on the line. When the right set-up is seen, that trader is ready and clicks the mouse. The genius, on the other hand, analyzes the market until the opportunity is gone. The average person scores again.

Yet another problem with the Doctrine of Genius is that many geniuses are single focused in their abilities. They can do one thing very, very well. But, often, they are not generalists. I think that good traders are generalists; at least in the skill sets that they possess. Trading requires a variety of skills. A good trader analyzes, executes, keeps emotions in check, and manages the risks and exercises good money management. The successful trader is the master of a wide array of skills.

Finally, I think there is one other reason that many geniuses have problems with the markets. They are not risk takers. They rarely ever had to take risks. In school, they knew the answer and they marked it. They knew how to put the widget together and they did it. They are just not used to a lot of the trial and error stuff that the rest of us have mastered. So, they are uncomfortable with risks. Trading is based on calculated risk and if you are adverse to risk, you cannot be a trader.

Now, do not take me wrong. I am not saying that successful traders like me are dummies. But, I realize that I am truly one of the average people. I make mistakes and I deal with them. I know that I do not always have the right answer so I am continuously searching for more information and more data to double check my analysis.

If you consider yourself a genius, don't give up, just assume a few of the characteristics of the rest of us. Realize that you are not always right. Analyze but don't analyze so much that you miss the big picture. Practice dealing with error—and maybe spend a little more time at the water cooler.

Glossary

Big Four I consider four indicators to be very important. I refer to these indicators as the Big Four. They consist of the S&P Futures, the Nasdaq Futures, the TTICK (an indicator that I designed), and the DAX Futures. Electronic trading on the DAX Futures ends at 1:00 P.M. Central Time. I replace the DAX with the Dow Futures as my fourth big indicator when the DAX closes.

CAC-40 The CAC is a stock exchange located in Paris that lists 40 French companies. There is both a CAC cash market and a futures market. CAC stands for Compagnie des Agents de Change 40 Index.

Cash markets The term cash market refers to the aggregate market value of the underlying securities upon which a futures contract is based. For example, S&P Cash refers to the aggregate market value of all the stocks traded on the S&P Index. Nasdaq Cash refers to the aggregate value of all the stocks traded on the Nasdaq Index.

CBOT The Chicago Board of Trade (CBOT) is an exchange located in Chicago. The Dow Futures and bond futures are traded at the CBOT. The CBOT has an electronic system known as the a/c/e that hosts electronic trading 20 hours a day for both the Dow Futures and bond futures.

CME The Chicago Mercantile Exchange (CME) is located in Chicago. S&P Futures and Nasdaq futures contracts are traded on this exchange. The CME has an electronic trading system known as the Globex. Electronic trading on the Globex is conducted virtually 24 hours a day.

DAX The DAX is a German index listed on the Frankfurt exchange. It is a very important foreign market and I consider it to be one of the Big Four. Trading on the DAX is possible through the Eurex. The currency used for trading the DAX is the euro.

Derivative   A derivative is a security that obtains its value from another underlying instrument. Futures contracts and options are two examples of derivatives. The value of an S&P Futures contract depends on the current market value of the S&P Cash Index. Likewise, the value of a stock option depends on the value of the stock upon which it is based. If IBM is trading at $100 a share and there is an option to buy at $90 a share, the value of the option is $10 per share. However, if IBM is trading at $85 a share, the same option is out-of-the-money and is worthless.

Exchange   An exchange is the place where securities are traded. The Chicago Board of Trade (CBOT), the Chicago Mercantile Exchange (CME), and the New York Stock Exchange (NYSE) are examples of exchanges.

FTSE   The FTSE is an exchange located in London. It is an important market during early morning trading.

Globex   The Globex is the electronic market operated by the Chicago Mercantile Exchange. The S&P Futures e-mini contracts are traded on the Globex and the big S&P 500 Futures contracts are traded on the Globex during the night market.

Grim Reaper   I refer to the time between 1:30 and 2:00 P.M. Central Time to be the Grim Reaper. During this time there is often a counter trend in the market. There may also be a lot of volatility and unpredictability. Protective stops are often hit, resulting in a loss. Therefore, I refer to this time as the Grim Reaper because it ushers in death for many trades.

Hang Seng   The Hang Seng is an exchange located in Hong Kong. I consider it to be an important market that can exert some degree of influence on U. S. markets, especially in the early hours of the night session.

Index   An index is a group of stocks that is deemed to be representative of a broader market. The Dow Jones Industrial Average is the oldest and most respected index in the United States. In theory, the health of this index reflects the overall health of the general market.

Key number   A key number is a number that is powerful in the market. It is a point where support or resistance is exerted. Some key numbers gain significance over time and are historically important, such as the 10,000 on the Dow. Every market has historical key numbers that are unique to that market. Other numbers are key numbers because they have exerted strength in recent trading. Examples of these key numbers are the yearly opening price, monthly opening price, daily opening price, and so forth.

Limit order   A limit order is a type of order that directs a broker to execute an order at a specified price or better. For example, a buy limit order sets a maximum price that a buyer will pay. The buyer will never pay more than that price. Likewise, a sell limit sets a minimum price at which a seller will sell. He will not get less than his limit price. *Limit orders are filled on a first come first served basis and there* *is no guarantee that a limit order will be filled.* For example, if a buyer places a buy limit order to purchase an S&P Futures contract at 1100.00 and there are already 100 orders to purchase the security at that same price, the new order will be 101 in line for execution. It will not be filled until all 100 of the previous orders waiting in line have been filled. If the price leaps up or falls back, the order may not be filled at all. This is the inherent risk of a limit order.

Margin   Margin basically means leverage. A futures account must be a margin account. To day trade stocks, one needs an equities margin account. A margin account allows a trader to leverage trading power by borrowing a portion of total funds from the broker. In this way, a trader gains the ability to control a greater amount of assets than the trading account balance would otherwise allow. The amount of margin that is required depends upon the security that is traded and other factors. Each exchange may set minimum margin requirements and brokers may set higher requirements. Futures are highly margined securities and the increased level of margin increases their risks.

Market order   An order that directs a broker to immediately execute a transaction at the best available price. This is the only type of order with guaranteed execution because it is guaranteed to be executed at the best available price at the time that the order reaches the trading floor.

Nasdaq   The Nasdaq is an exchange that is totally electronic. There is both a Nasdaq cash market and a Nasdaq Futures market.

Nikkei   The Nikkei is an exchange that is located in Tokyo, Japan. When the Nikkei and other Asian markets open, it is the early evening hours in the United States, and most U.S. traders are winding down from their trading day.

Options   An option gives the buyer the right but not the obligation to buy or sell a specific security at a predetermined price, on or before a certain date. For that right, the buyer of the option pays a fee. If the preset transaction price or strike price is hit, the option may be exercised. If the strike price is hit the option is said to be in-the-money. If the strike price is not hit the option is out-of-the-money and expires useless on the expiration date.

Pivot   A pivot is a point at which the market shifts. Pivot numbers are points of support and resistance. These points are key numbers in the market. Above the pivot point is bullish; below the pivot point is bearish.

Protective stop   A protective stop is an order that is placed in an attempt to limit the risk of a trade. A trader determines the maximum loss that he or she is willing to take on the trade and sets a protective stop at that point. Even though a stop is placed, there is no guarantee that it will be filled. In rare circumstances, the market may move very quickly and the stop order may be passed over and not executed. In such a case, the trader may lose more than anticipated. In the case of a futures contract, the trader may lose more than the value of the entire trading account. If the account balance falls below the margin requirements, the trader receives a margin call for the additional loss.

Real time quotes   Real time quotes are price data that are timely and accurate. These quotes should be as timely as electronically possible. That is, they should be nearly up-to-the-second accurate. There are various hardware and software packages that provide real time quotes. Delayed quotes are often available free of charge but are unreliable. Real time quotes are needed to successfully day trade and this information is not free.

Reference bar   A reference bar is a bar that is formed by trading during a specified period of time. I use 30-minute reference bars. Specifically, I use the bars formed from 3:30 to 4:00 P.M.; 2:30 to 3:00 A.M.; 8:30 to 9:00 A.M.; and 12:30 to 1:00 P.M. I call these bars reference bars because I use them as points of reference for specific time periods. If the market trades above the bar, I consider the market bullish; if it trades below the reference bar, I consider it bearish. For example, I use the bar formed between 8:30 and 9:00 A.M. to assist me with my morning trading and I use the bar formed between 12:30 and 1:00 P.M. to assist me with my afternoon trading.

Resistance   Resistance is a point that the market has trouble trading above. Sellers step into the market at this point and take profits. Therefore, the market has to exhibit a degree of strength to break resistance and trade higher.

Rollover day   A futures contract differs from a stock or equity in that futures contracts expire quarterly. The contract for each quarter is identified by an assigned letter as follows: March (H), June (M), September (U), and December (Z). The second Thursday of the month of a quarter is rollover day. On that day, trading begins on the next quarter's contracts. For example, the second Thursday of March begins trading on June contracts; the second Thursday of June begins trading on September contracts, etc. Generally, trading on the previous quarter expires on the third Thursday of the month of the rollover, for example, the third Thursday in March is the last day to trade March contracts and the third Thursday in June is the last day to trade June contracts. Once trading begins on the new contracts, liquidity in the old contracts falls dramatically as traders shift from the expiring contracts to the new contracts. Therefore, it is wise to trade the new contracts once rollover day has arrived.

Scalp trade   A type of short term trading that attempts to profit from small price changes.

Slippage   Sometimes a trader attempts to buy or sell a contract at a specific price, but the order is executed at a different price. The amount of difference between the desired price and the confirmed or executed price is the slippage. One often receives some slippage from a stop order. The way to avoid slippage is to use limit orders. For example, a trader places a stop order at 1147.00, but the order is executed at 1147.50. The trader suffered a half point of slippage.

Stop order   An order given to a broker that becomes a market order when the market price of the underlying instrument reaches or exceeds the specific price stated. Slippage may occur with stop orders.

Support   A point at which buyers step into a falling market. When buyers step in, the downward momentum is stopped or slowed down.

Tick   The smallest increment that a price can fluctuate. In the S&P 500 futures contract, each tick equals 0.10 points. There are ten ticks in one point. For the e-mini, each tick equals 0.25 points. There are four ticks in one point. For the Dow Jones futures contract, each tick is equal to one point.

TTICK   A proprietary indicator created by Tom Busby that combines the price action of the S&P futures and the TICK (New York Stock Exchange Indicator) to help determine the strength/weakness of the market.

Tilt number   This is the largest amount of money that a trader is willing to risk per contract, per trade, or per day. A trader should determine a tilt number in advance and stick to it. If a trader loses the amount of the tilt number in a trade, he or she should exit the trade. If the trader loses the daily tilt number at any time during the day, he or she should stop trading for the day. By observing the tilt number, the trader preserves capital on those days when either the market or the trader is not functioning as expected.

TICK   A market indicator that reflects the difference between the number of issues trading down from the number of issues trading up on the New York Stock Exchange. The TICK is a leading indicator for market direction. A reading of +1,000 or so indicates that the market is over bought; a reading of −1,000 or so indicates that the market is over sold.

Trade zone   A period of time identified by Tom Busby as a time when there tends to be greater volatility and liquidity in the market. Trading opportunities are generally more abundant during a trade zone. There are three trade zones during the 24-hour trading day.

Triple Witching Day   The Friday after the third Thursday of the contract expiration month. On this day, the futures contracts, future options contracts, and equities options contracts all expire.

TRIN   The TRIN, which is also known as the Arms Index or Trading Index, measures volatility. The TRIN is a ratio of ratios. It is calculated as follows:

$$\frac{\text{Advancing Issues/Declining Issues}}{\text{Advancing Volume/Declining Volume}}$$

A TRIN of 1.0 is considered neutral. The lower the TRIN, the more bullish the indication, the higher the TRIN the more bearish. Like the TICK, the TRIN is a short-term indicator. The TRIN works inversely to the TICK. As the TICK goes up, the TRIN goes down and as the TICK moves down, the TRIN goes up.

V-Factor   A proprietary indicator created by Tom Busby to monitor volume on specific indexes or exchanges and to reflect that volume in a ratio of buys to sells.

Volatility   The trading range of a particular commodity or security for a specified period of time.

Volume   Total number of units of a security traded during any given time period.

Getting Started

COMPUTER EQUIPMENT, TRADING PLATFORMS, AND OTHER ESSENTIALS

The game has changed a lot since I started playing it. Back in the 1980s, there were no discount brokers, no online trading, no two- or three-second order fills. Every trader didn't have a computer with access to mountains of information at his fingertips. Orders were called into the clearing houses and everything took time. I'm not a computer person, but if I wanted to keep on top I had to learn enough to survive. There is a real generation gap between me and younger traders. They grew up with a mouse in their hands and they are very comfortable with technology and its advances. I survived because I have had a lot of people help me and because I wanted to play the game and win. If you want to be a successful day trader today, you must take advantage of the huge technological advances that have been made.

In this appendix, I go through the steps to take in order to get started as a day trader. If you are already trading, you may not need this information because it is very basic. You probably already know it, and hopefully you like the set-up that you have. Therefore, you probably want to just skim this information to see if anything in it may be new to you.

What Do You Want to Trade?

The first issue that you must resolve is what trading vehicle you will trade. If you want to trade futures, you must open a margin account. If you want to trade equities, you need an equities account, and if you want to day trade equities, you need a margined equity account. Recall that when I opened my first brokerage account, I intended to trade pork bellies, a commodity. Yet, I opened an equities account. I did not know the difference. Some traders are more comfortable with one vehicle while others prefer another. I like futures, but many traders only want to trade equities. Still other traders prefer options, or commodities, or bonds. Think about the particular characteristics of the item that you are trading. Do you have the personality for trading it? Do you have the education and knowledge that you need or can you acquire the necessary knowledge? How much capital is needed? How much time? Consider your answers carefully and select what you want to trade.

I have known some people who were very good at trading one thing and very bad at trading another. For example, some folks just seem to really understand the equities market while others seem to intuitively grasp options. It really doesn't matter what you select; just as long as it matches your skills and your resources. After deciding what you will trade, immerse yourself in it and learn all that you can. In this game, knowledge really is power. And, of course be sure that you open the type of account that you need in order to trade the vehicle of your choice.

Get Educated

Do not try to trade without getting educated. Start by reading and researching. The bookshelves are lined with books on all aspects of trading. You, however, must know that because you are reading this one. Also, there are many courses that are taught online and at various cites around the United States and around the world.

At DTI, we teach courses in Mobile, AL and in other major U. S. cities. There are a number of other programs and courses taught by very experienced traders. The Chicago Board of Trade (CBOT) offers educational materials and so does the Chicago Mercantile Exchange (CME). Some brokerage firms offer training also. Just be careful and don't believe anyone who tells you that you will get rich quick with no risk and no loss. Some people have systems that can beat Wall Street. At least that is the claim. Be very careful about that because there is no system that will work in all phases of the markets. You must be educated and change as the environment changes. That is the only way to stay on top.

Remember that education is not cheap so plan to allot some financial resources to education.

Open an Account

Next, you need both a brokerage firm and a clearing house. A brokerage firm places your trades for you but the clearing house transacts them or clears them through the exchanges. Today, there are so many companies out there offering so many types of services. Some offer very low commissions and have low margin requirements. Other firms charge greater commissions and may require greater margins. Still other companies may cost a little more but offer a wider array of services and assistance. Check to get the best deal that you can. Shop around because there are some really good deals out there. Once you start trading, the commission structure and other costs of your trades is very important to you. Commissions will eat you up if you overtrade.

In addition to cost, find out how statements are received, what type of support the company has, and who to contact if there is a problem. Believe me, there will very likely be times when you will have a problem, technological or otherwise, and need to contact either the broker or the clearing house. Be sure that you know what to do when these times arise. Get emergency numbers and keep them at your fingertips for easy access.

Remember that if you want to trade futures you need a margin account. To trade equities, get an equity account, and to day trade equities or options, you need a margin equities account. Be sure that you have the correct account to meet your needs.

A Computer

When you trade you need a computer that can handle the vast amount of data coming through it. You will be receiving real time quotes and executing trades. You do not want your computer to freeze up when orders are in the market. I have had that happen to me and it is not a good feeling. Therefore, you need to be sure that your computer can handle the huge quantity of data and other programs that will be required.

I confess that I do not know a lot about computers, but Geof Smith, my Chief Instructor knows a great deal. He grew up with a mouse in his hand and he keeps me informed about what I need. Therefore, I will give you an overview of the basic equipment required. Technology changes daily. At the time of this writing (May 2005), I recommend that you use at least a 2.6 GHz or higher or its equivalent Pentium 4 or equivalent processor. You need at least 1 GB of RAM.

You also need a video card so that you can operate two or more monitors at the same time. When you have various markets that you are monitoring and charts that you are observing, it is handy to have at least two monitors. That is not to say that you can't trade with one monitor, you can. I use one monitor when I travel. But, two is just a little more convenient.

I suggest that your hard drive have at least 40 giga bytes of hard drive with 7,200 RPM SATA drive, with 8 MB cache. This allows for faster reading and writing.

You can either get a hyper-threaded processor or a computer with two processors. You need this in order to run two processes at the same time.

Also, you must have at least one monitor. Get at least a 17-inch flat screen. You may want more.

Finally, you will need to have a LAN port for proper broadband access. I actually know of a few people who trade without a high-speed internet connection. They still rely on modem access. I do not recommend that you do it. The market moves too quickly and you want to be able to move with it. Therefore, get a high-speed connection. You can either get DSL through your telephone provider or cable through your cable provider. Just be sure that the service you get is reliable. Nothing is more irritating than being in a trade and having your cable or telephone connection go down. You will be scrambling to call your broker to take your trade to the market or check your stops. I've been there. You do not want to be. Another option is to have your trading computer custom built. A friend of mine, John Chittenden at www.xview. com, has built several computers for me over the years. He takes all of the guesswork out of what a trader truly needs in a computer.

Get a Trading Platform

Next, you need a trading platform. There are many companies that offer them, and they have a lot of different capabilities and services that may come with them. They also come with a variety of cost structures. Again, shop around and get your best deal. You may be surprised by what is out there.

Once you get a platform, practice using it. For at least a week do simulations. Learn how to enter orders and how to exit positions quickly. Some platforms have a flatten button that allows you to exit all of your positions with the click of that one button. Other platforms allow orders to be executed in a preprogrammed manner. There are all sorts of possibilities.

One of the most common mistakes of traders is making an error with the trading platform. It is so easy to click on the wrong side of the trading dome and sell when you mean to buy or vise versa. That is why you need to practice on your program before you trade real contracts. Do many simulations and practice placing orders, changing orders, moving orders, and checking order status. Be sure that you are comfortable with the process and that you are able to get into and out of the market very quickly.

Data Feed

You cannot trade unless you have the correct data. You need a real time quote system that brings you accurate and timely information. Be sure that your data provider can get you the information you need for what you are trading. Some sources do not offer futures data, others may handle futures but not equities. Some may offer data from domestic markets, but not foreign exchanges. Be sure that you will get the data that you need.

The cost of data feed depends on what you get. There is a base fee charged by the exchanges so the more you get the more you pay.

It is critical that the data you receive are reliable. There are some sites that offer free data, but it is delayed information. I know of no site that offers free real time quotes. You have to pay for it, but it is worth it. You just cannot afford to trade using old data. The markets can move at breathtaking speed and you have to know the real numbers. Also, some data feed providers are just not as reliable as others. Ask around and find out what other traders have to say. Then, select the provider that offers you what you need reliably.

Quote and Charting Program

You may want a quote and charting program that will accept data that you receive. I use RoadMap software. It can create charts and do all sorts of other functions for me like storing data and other things. You probably will want some sort of program. Again, there are a lot of them out there. Research and find out what is best for you.

A Few Other Thoughts

In addition to having the right equipment, you need the right time and space. Find a place that is quiet so that you can concentrate. Trading requires concentration. If you are distracted, you may miss some important data or information. You need to be focused on the task at hand—making money.

Also, day trading profits and losses are governed by specific and particular IRS rules. Therefore, get a CPA who knows about trading and can properly handle your taxes. This is very important so be sure to inquire about the knowledge that your tax preparation specialist has in this area.

CHECK LIST FOR TRADING

1. Decide what you want to trade.
2. Get educated. Learn about the investment of your choice.
3. Open an account.
4. Get a computer that is powerful enough to handle trading requirements.
5. Select a trading platform and spend many hours practicing on that platform. Be sure that you know how to enter and exit the market quickly.

6. Purchase reliable data. Be sure that your data are timely and accurate.

7. Find a quote and charting program that meets your needs. This will probably not be free.

8. Allocate time for trading.

9. Locate a quiet place where you can trade and concentrate with a minimum of distraction.

10. Be certain that your CPA knows the tax laws regarding day trading and that your tax filings are handled correctly.

Order Types

U nderstanding and placing orders can be confusing. None of us were born with a mouse in our hands, and it is easy to accidentally enter the wrong type of order or click on the wrong side of the trading dome. Therefore, before you start trading you need to become very familiar with order types and you need to practice placing orders in simulated situations. Making mistakes in order placement can turn an otherwise profitable trade into a major loser. Every trader has made a mistake by placing the wrong type of order and suffered financially because of it.

If you trade different indices simultaneously, you might even enter the wrong market because the domes all look remarkably alike. I remember one day recently when I intended to trade the S&P Index Futures. Don't ask me how I did it, but I actually placed a trade for Japanese yen. Seconds after I made the trade I realized that something was wrong. It took me a few seconds to figure out that I had just bought the yen. I stopped everything else and focused on getting out of that market.

By sheer luck, I actually was profitable on the trade, but even if I had lost money, I would have taken the trade to the market. I never want to be in a market accidentally. I always plan, prepare, and strategize. My point, however, is that even experienced traders make mistakes when placing orders. Therefore, it is very important that you learn all you can about order placement and practice the process before you ever begin trading. This will minimize your errors and should help you improve your profits.

Now let's get down to order placement.

Orders allow traders to do two things: get into the market and get out of the market. A buy order is an order to go long or to cover or exit a short position. A sell order is an order to go short or to cover or exit a long position. A buy stop order and as sell limit order must be placed above the current market price. A sell stop and a buy limit must be placed below the market price. What happens if you make a mistake and electronically place a sell limit order below the point where the market is trading? Your order becomes a market order and immediately goes to the market. The same thing happens if you place a buy limit order above the price where the market is trading. The order becomes a market order and immediately takes you into the market at the current price.

Why is this a problem? Assume that the S&P 500 Index Futures is trading at 1005.00 and you are long (you bought the market at 1003.00). You want to take profit when the market reaches 1007.00. You move your cursor to the trading dome and click below the point where the market is currently trading. At that point, your order becomes a market order and is immediately executed. You meant to place a sell limit at 1007.00, two points above the current market price. Unfortunately, you clicked the mouse at the wrong point. Instead of getting the 4 points of profit you worked for, you only made 2 points because you made a foolish error with your order placement.

Or, the S&P is trading at 1004.00. You want to enter the market if it goes up to 1005.75. You want to buy a contract if the market can rise to that level. If it cannot, you intend to stay out of the market. You preplace your order, but accidentally you enter a limit order instead of a stop order. Again, the order immediately goes to the market and you have entered the market at a point at which you did not intend. The market may not rise to your anticipated entry point resulting in a loss for you. The following sections review the basic order types.

Market Order

A market order is an order given to a broker for immediate execution at the best price available when the order reaches the exchange. A market order is the only order with guaranteed execution. When placing any order, remember that the bid price is the price the buyer is willing to pay, and the ask price is the price at which the seller is willing to sell. Expect some slippage with market orders, especially in a rapidly moving market.

Stop Orders

A stop order is an order that becomes a market order when the market price of the underlying instrument reaches or exceeds the specific price stated. This is a hold, or contingency, order that will not be elected until the market reaches a specific price. Execution of the order is contingent on the market hitting the price. This type of order can be used to preposition an order for market entry, or to set your order for protection. There may be slippage with this type of order. Remember that the execution of this order is not guaranteed because your price may not be reached and your order may not be filled.

Stop-Limit Orders

This type of order is a combination between a stop order and a limit order. The trader first specifies the stop price (the price at which the order becomes elected), then specifies the limit price. This type of order puts a hold on a limit order. When the stop price is hit, the order becomes a limit order.

Market if Touched (MIT)

This order may be used instead of a limit order. Remember that when you place a limit order, you are not guaranteed a fill unless the market trades through the specified price that you have set. However, with an MIT order, the order goes directly to the floor as a market order once the specified price is hit. Therefore, if the price is hit, the order is immediately executed.

Order Cancels Order (OCO)

Some trading platforms allow OCO orders and others do not. With this type of order, a trader can place more than one order at the same time. If one of the orders is executed, the other order is automatically cancelled. For example, if you want to go long (buy) an S&P e-mini at 1122.00, you want to take profits at 1125.00, and you want to enter your protective stop at 1119.25, you may be best served by placing an OCO order. You buy at 1122.00 and you are long. If your profit target is 1125.00 and your order is hit, the 1119.25 order is pulled and you are out of the market with profit and no orders sitting on the books. Or, if the trade goes against you and the market goes down to 1119.25, the protective stop is hit and you are out of the market with a loss. However, the profit target order of 1125.00 is cancelled. Therefore, you do not have to worry about an order sitting on the books that could later be executed without your knowledge. Traders often use OCO orders during the late night and early morning hours.

A Note on Slippage

When an order is placed, the order may not be executed at the desired price. For example, you may wish to buy IBM at $90.00 per share. You place a stop order to buy at that price. However, your order is not filled at $90.00, but at $90.10. You had slippage of ten cents per share on your order. When possible, use limit orders to reduce slippage.

Suggested Reading

Borsellino, Lewis. *The Day Trader: From the Pit to the PC*. John Wiley & Sons, 1999.

Kiyosaki, Robert T. *Rich Dad's Prophecy: Why the Biggest Stock Market Crash in History is Still Coming... and How You Can Prepare Yourself and Profit From It!* Warner Books, 2004.

Livermore, Jesse. *How to Trade in Stocks: The Livermore Formula for Combining Time Element and Price*. Traders Press, 1991.

Roosevelt, Ruth Barrons. *12 Habitudes of Highly Successful Traders*. Traders Press, 2001.

Schwager, Jack D. *New Market Wizards*. HarperBusiness, 1992.

Smitten, Richard. *Jesse Livermore: The World's Greatest Stock Trader*. Traders Press, 1999.

Helpful Websites

Barchart, *www.barchart.com*. Collects average true range data for futures and stock and offers much more valuable information and data.

Barrons, *www.barrons.com*. Scheduled news reports. *Trader* column is beneficial and interesting.

Chicago Board of Trade, *www.cbot.com*. Overview of all CBOT products along with free educational seminars.

Chicago Board Options Exchange, *www.cboe.com*. Overview of CBOE products. Great source for options information.

Chicago Mercantile Exchange, *www.cme.com*. Overview of all CME products along with free educational seminars.

Cornerstone Investors Network, *www.cornerstoneinvestorsnetwork.com*. This is an investment club based in Chicago and Florida. Conducts free educational seminars online.

CyberTrader, *www.cybertrader.com*. Offers online stock execution. Leader in the industry.

Daily FX, *www.dailyfx.com*. Offers global financial news in order of currencies.

DTI, *www.dtitrader.com*. Weekly scheduled news reports and educational information.

Eurex & Eurex US, *www.eurex.com* and *www.eurexus.com*. Overview of Eurex and Eurex US products, specifically the German DAX Futures (Eurex) and the Russell Indexes (Eurex US).

Hans-Engelbrecht, *www.hans-engelbrecht.com.* Offers quotes for the 30 stocks that makeup the DAX futures index that trade on the Frankfurt Exchange.

Wall Street Journal, *www.wsj.com.* Current news on stocks. *Heard It On the Street* column is beneficial.

World Wide Traders, *www.worldwidetraders.com.* A California based educational Investment Club. Free educational seminars online.

Xview Computer Builders, *www.xview.com.* Delivers computers ready-to-go, with all software installed. Trader-specific machines available.

Index

A

Account balance, management, 164
a/c/e (electronic trading system), 23
Afternoon trading, opportunities, 21
Arbitrary stops, 92
Arrogance, disadvantage, 65–66, 162
ATR. *See* Average true range
Average true range (ATR), 126–127

B

Bankruptcy, filing, 3
Bar charts (30-minute charts), usage,
    39–41
Bear markets, strategy (need), 4–5
Bigger Fool Theory, 3–4
Black Monday (10/19/87), 5
    1929 crash, comparison, 6
    crash/correction, 6
    psychological pain, 12
Bond futures, trading, 128–129
    checklist, 129
Breaking news, impact, 99–100, 102
Bull markets, strategy (need), 4–5
Bureau of Economic Analysis, 105
Bureau of Labor Statistics, 106
Business
    cost, determination, 86
    media coverage, 152

C

CAC, 157
Capital, preservation, 96–97
CCI. *See* Consumer Confidence Index

Chicago Board of Trade (CBOT), 23
    websites, 136
Chicago Mercantile Exchange (CME)
    electronic order entry system, 23
    exit positions, 101
    websites, 136
Combination stops, 92
Commissions
    calculation, 17
    variation, 86
Commodities
    impact, 35
    key numbers, usage, 33, 35
    trading, 2
Computer systems, disadvantages, 6
Confirmation, 116
Construction spending, 107–108
Consumer Confidence Board, 107
Consumer Confidence Index (CCI),
    106–107
Consumer Price Index (CPI),
    105–106

D

Daily numbers, understanding, 37–38
DAX, 157
    daily opening, 24
    monitoring, 22–23
    trading, 114
DAX Futures, 113, 149
    Index, 24
        tracking, 159
    movement, 52

DAX Futures, *continued*
  number, importance, 39
  trading, 135, 151
Day trading
  business, 85–87
  criticism, 96
  stocks, 125
Day Trading Institute (DTI), 87, 155
  accountability system, 97
  cardinal rule, 91
  initiation, 13
  instruction, 165
Deviation, calculation, 120–121
Diversification, 119–120, 131
Doctrine of Genius, 169
  problem, 171
  untruth, 170
Dow Futures Index
  key numbers, 41
  tracking, 159
Dow Jones Industrial Average,
    decline, 1
Dynamic market, 82–83

E
Early Bird Trade, criteria, 148
ECI. *See* Employment Cost Index
E.F. Hutton, 9
Emotions
  impact. *See* Trading
  power, 161–162
  taming, 162
Employer conflicts, 7–8
Employment Cost Index (ECI), 109
Entry prices, 149–150
Equities
  account, opening, 2
  markets, overvaluation, 133
  trading, 96
  usage. *See* Risk
Exit plans, 67–68

F
Fear, impact, 79, 161–162
Federal Open Market Committee
    (FOMC), 103
  press releases, 104

Federal Reserve, 109
  interest rates, decrease, 101
  reports/announcements, 103–105
  website, 136
Financial loss, 6
Financial markets
  flux, 17
  freefall (10/19/87), 1
Financial news, 152
Financial opportunities, 9
FOMC. *See* Federal Open Market
    Committee
FTSE, 157
Futures. *See* Standard & Poor's Futures
  contracts, control, 134
  indices, 127
    trading, 4–5
    usage, 124
  market, key numbers (impact), 35
  trading, risks (knowledge), 94–95

G
GDP. *See* Gross domestic product
Geniuses. *See* Doctrine of Genius
  analysis. *See* Market
  consideration, 172
  varieties, 169
Global time, attention, 29
Globex, 23
  electronic trading, 101
  high/low, 38
  market, timing. *See* Standard &
    Poor's
Gold trading, 130–131
  checklist, 131
Greed, impact, 63–64, 79, 165
Green Circle Country, 97, 155
Greenspan, Alan, 37
  impact, 104
  public statements, impact, 99
Grim Reaper time, 58, 156
Gross domestic product (GDP), 105

H
Hang Seng, 157
  closure, 1
  market, daily opening, 23

Holidays
  attention, 157
  significance, 27
Housing starts, 108
Hussein, Saddam (capture), 102

I
Ignorance, danger, 24
Index funds, 120–121
Index futures, trading, 49–50, 131–132
Index stocks, 122
Indexes, trading, 114
Indicators, 90–91
  information, 115–116
  support, 160
Information/data, interpretation, 46, 48
Institute of Supply Management (ISM), 108–109
Investment portfolio, sale, 8

K
Key numbers, 32–33
  collection, 115
  impact. *See* Futures
  learning, observation (usage), 44
  stocks, respect, 33
  stops, 92
  usage, 36–37, 158–159. *See also* Commodities; Market; Profits; Protective stops

L
Liquidation, 8
Liquidity, significance, 19
Livermore, Jesse, 15–17, 31–32, 141
London Financial Times Stock Exchange, decline, 1
Long-term traders, 139–140
Losing streak, breaking, 28
Losses
  control, 89
  targets, 94

M
Margin requirements, 95
Market. *See* Dynamic market

analysis, 41
bullish overtone, 51–52
conditions, analysis, 140
context, 114–115
correction, 67
direction
  reconsideration, 27
  understanding, 136–137
entry
  key numbers, usage, 42–43, 53
  preparation, 137
genius analysis, 170
investigation, 159–160
movement, 57
  people, impact, 18
moving reports, 166
numbers, collection, 147–148
opening price, 26
reset button, 39
response, 48
reversal, 81
shift, 145
strategic attack, 77, 83
study, 15
trading, 156–157
unpredictability, 91
volatility, 20
Market-tested strategy, learning, 13
MCSI. *See* Michigan Consumer Sentiment Index
Media commentary, 147
Media coverage. *See* Business
Mental stops, reliance, 69
Merrill Lynch, confidence, 4
Metamorphosis, 9–10
Michigan Consumer Sentiment Index (MCSI), 106–107
Mistakes
  identification, 167
  review, 10–11
Money
  loss, experience, 8
  management, 164
Morning activity, impact. *See* Trading
Moving average, 129–130, 132

Moving news events, impact, 100–103
Mutual funds, trading checklist, 121

N

Naked options, sale, 132
Nasdaq Futures, tracking, 159
New York Stock Exchange (NYSE), 45
    issues, 81, 160
        indicators, 54
New York Tick (TICK), 54–55,
        115–116, 160
News. *See* Financial news
    events, 110, 116, 165–166
    expectations, 149
    impact, 127. *See also* Breaking news
Nikkei, 157
    daily opening, 23
    decline, 1

O

OEX Exchange, index options trades,
        146
Oil trading
    checklist, 130
    option strategy, usage, 129–130
Opening price, impact, 36
Optimism, advantages, 8–9
Options
    approach, 37
    concentration, 5
    trading, success, 4
Overtrading, 137–138
    prevention, strategy, 17

P

Past, usage/improvement, 140–141
Patience, advantage, 16
Penn Square banking crisis, 9
Persistence, 7–9
Personal situation, evaluation, 88
Pessimism, disadvantages, 12
Pork bellies, trading, 2
Position, liquidation, 64–65
PPI. *See* Producer Price Index
Pre-Paid Legal (PPD), 16
Preparation, absence, 133
Present trading, 137–138

Prices, reading. *See* Stocks
Problem solving, 11
Producer Price Index (PPI), 106
Profits
    focus, 12–13
    targets, setting, 68, 94
        key numbers, usage, 43
Protective stops
    impact, 127
    placements, 20–21, 83, 130.
        See also Resistance levels;
        Support levels
    determination, 91
        key numbers, usage, 43
    pulling, 126
    usage, 68–69, 78

Q

QQQQ, 122

R

Real time quotes, 46
Real-time market numbers, 147–148
Recession, signs, 107
Resistance levels, 115
    protective stop placements, 65
Risk
    calculation, 161
    control, 127
    involvement, 165
    knowledge, 89–90
    level, 87–89
    limitation, 93
    management, 12–13, 85, 87
        equities, usage, 95–96
    positioning, 20
    taking, 90–91
    tolerance, evaluation, 85–87
    understanding, 95
RoadMap, 22–23, 69
    software, 92

S

Sectors, identification, 119–120
September 11th (2001), effects, 100, 102
Short-term traders, 139–140
Smith, Bobby Gene, 16

Smith, Geof, 88, 100–101
Smitten, Richard, 16, 32
Standard & Poor's (S&P)
  500
    correlation, 125
    opening price, 120
  100 puts, 5
  Globex market, opening, 151–152
Standard & Poor's (S&P) Futures
  daily morning initiation, 20
  e-mini contracts, 64, 100
  Index
    tracking, 159
    trading, 40, 42
  initiation, 4
  movement, 52
  numbers, 42
  opening monthly price, 36–37
  opening price, 26
  trading, 9
  understanding, 113
Stock market crash (10/19/87), 167
  theories, 2
Stocks
  holding, charges, 127
  investment, 123–124
  prices, reading, 52–53, 160
  purchase, 3
  quotes
    attention, 3
    reading, 59
  respect. *See* Key numbers
  selection, 122–123
  trading, 33, 121–123
    checklist, 128
Stops. *See* Arbitrary stops;
      Combination stops; Key
      numbers; Protective stops;
      Volatility
Strategy reversal, 35
Support levels, protective stop
      placements, 65
Survival, 7–9

T
Tactical issues, 80–82
Tape reading

accuracy, 49, 159
  importance, 46
  skill, 53
  time, impact, 160
Technology, 135–136, 166
Terrorist attacks, 165
  effects (9/11/2001), 100, 102
TICK. *See* New York Tick
Ticks, 77–79, 156, 163–164
  usage, 79–80
Tilt number, establishment, 89
Time
  consideration, 115
  impact, 28. *See also* Tape reading
  30-minute frames, 40
  usage. *See* Trading
Timeout, impact, 158
Timing, importance, 29–30
Traders
  mediocrity, 140
  strategy, need, 162–163
Trades, 77–79, 156, 163–164
  goals, 97–98
  limiting, 17
  prices, determination, 117–119
  recording, 140–141
  time, determination, 117–118
  timing, 150–151
  usage, 79–80
  zones, 22, 58
Trading. *See* Present trading
  active times, advantage, 19–20
  asset, 134
  avocation, 3
  buddy, usage, 143
  conditions, morning activity
      (impact), 20–21
  diary
    discipline/usage, 142–143
    recording, 141
  education, 143–144
  element, time (usage), 28–29
  emotions, impact, 70–71
  global movement, 23
  goals, 62–64, 81, 141–142
  24-hour clock, usage, 29–30
  losing, 66–67

Trading, *continued*
  methods, 31–32
    development, 13
  mistakes, 171
  opportunities. *See* Afternoon trading
  opposites, 29
  patterns, knowledge, 35
  plan, 73–76
    strategy, 76–77
  post-day session, 25
  preparation, 143–144
  profitability, 163–164
  progression, 38
  psychological game, 9
  session, 40–41
    closing, 21–22
  skills, 61
  strategy, execution, 80–82, 164
  style, 146–147
  success, 59
  three Ts, 77–79, 156
  time
    patterns, 18–19
    sensitivity, 156
  timing, knowledge, 16–17
  waiting, 15

  weakness, 93, 137–138
Trading Index (TRIN) (Arms Index),
    55, 81, 160
Trends, 77–79, 156, 163–164
  lines, 157
    example, 50–51
  usage, 79–80
TRIN. *See* Trading Index
TTICK, 56–58, 116, 160
Two-minute rule, 69

U
University of Michigan, 109
U.S. Department of Commerce, 108
U.S. Department of Labor, 106, 109

V
V-factor, 56, 160
Volatility
  significance, 19
  stops, 92
Volume, importance, 56

W
Wall Street, rationality/confidence, 18
Wilson, Woodrow, 103